H-G DEC 11 '89

D1011205

921    *Black Hist. coll.*
JOHNSON                                    ✓
GURALNICK, PETER.
SEARCHING FOR ROBERT JOHNSON.

DEMCO

# SEARCHING
# FOR
# ROBERT
# JOHNSON

ALSO BY PETER GURALNICK

*Sweet Soul Music*
*Lost Highway*
*Feel Like Going Home*

*Nighthawk Blues*

# SEARCHING FOR ROBERT JOHNSON

◆

## PETER GURALNICK

PRODUCED BY TOBY BYRON / MULTIPRISES

A DUTTON **O**belisk BOOK

E.P. DUTTON ◆ NEW YORK

FRONTISPIECE: *Robert Johnson, ca. 1935.*
COURTESY OF STEVE LAVERE, © 1989.

Copyright © 1989 by Toby Byron/Multiprises
Text copyright © 1982, 1989 by Peter Guralnick
All rights reserved. Printed in the U.S.A.

No part of this publication may be reproduced or transmitted in any form
or by any means, electronic or mechanical, including photocopy,
recording, or any information storage and retrieval system now known or
to be invented, without permission in writing from the publisher, except
by a reviewer who wishes to quote brief passages in connection with a
review written for inclusion in a magazine, newspaper, or broadcast.

Published in the United States by Obelisk Books, E. P. Dutton,
a division of Penguin Books USA Inc.,
2 Park Avenue, New York, N.Y. 10016.

Published simultaneously in Canada
by Fitzhenry and Whiteside, Limited, Toronto.

Library of Congress Cataloging-in-Publication Data

Guralnick, Peter.
Searching for Robert Johnson.

"Produced by Toby Byron/Multiprises"
"A Dutton Obelisk book"
Bibliography: p.
Discography: p.
1. Johnson, Robert, d. 1938.  2. Blues musicians—
Mississippi—Biography.  I. Title.
ML420.J735G8  1989        782.42164'3'092        89-7912
ISBN: 0-525-24801-3

Designed by Susan Marsh

1 3 5 7 9 10 8 6 4 2

FIRST EDITION

*For Sam Charters, Mack McCormick, and Chris Strachwitz,*
*who introduced me to the blues through their work . . .*
*and for my friend Bob Smith,*
*who leapt at the invitation.*

**W**HEN I WAS A FRESHMAN in college, in 1961–62, my most precious possessions were my blues records and a portable stereo phonograph which my mother had uncharacteristically purchased with green stamps. From time to time I read and reread Samuel Charters's pioneering *The Country Blues*, published in 1959, for its poetic descriptions of a music that seemed as remote as Kurdistan and destined always to remain so. I had perhaps fifty albums of country blues—Lightnin' Hopkins, Big Bill Broonzy, Blind Lemon Jefferson, Furry Lewis—it seemed as if there could scarcely be any more. Names that are as familiar as presidents' today, touchstones for anyone familiar with the roots of contemporary music, were the exclusive province of collectors then. My friends and I studied the little that was available, attempted to piece together virtually indecipherable lyrics, pored over each precious photograph, constructed a world of experience and feeling from elliptical clues. Of all the figures who beckoned to us from a remote, mysterious, and foreign past—certainly it was a past that was not our own—Robert Johnson stood out, tantalized, really, in a way that no other myth or archetype has ever done. Lightnin' Hopkins, the first real blues singer I had ever seen *live*, was, in Charters's words, "the last of the great blues singers," but the ethos of Robert Johnson was nowhere near so prosaic. "Almost nothing," Charters wrote in a chapter that consisted for the most part of song quotes, lyrical tormented quotes, "is known about his life. . . . He is only a name on a few recordings. . . . The finest of Robert Johnson's blues have a brooding sense of torment and despair. . . . His singing becomes so disturbed it is almost impossible to understand the words. The voice and the guitar rush in an incessant rhythm. As he sings he seems to cry out in a high falsetto voice."

What could be more appropriate to our sense of romantic mystery than an "emotionally disturbed" poet scarcely able to contain his "brooding sense of torment and despair"? Just as we imagined that Tommy McClennan was mad from the ferocity of his growl, that Blind Willie McTell was the unlikely reincarnation of a latter-day Flying Dutchman with his uncanny ability to turn up in the recording studio at least once in every decade, so Robert Johnson became the personification of the existential blues singer, unencumbered by corporeality or history, a fiercely incandescent spirit who had escaped the bonds of tradition by the sheer thrust of genius. Incredibly, all of this apostrophizing was based solely on Charters's chapter and one recorded selection, "Preachin' Blues," on which Johnson sounded somewhat thin, constricted, and out of control.

That is why I remember so vividly walking into Sam Goody's on 49th Street in New York, riffling through the blues section with a practiced eye, and discovering to my utter amazement (for there had been no announcement that I knew about; there was no place where you could conceivably *read* about such things) not one but two altogether unanticipated treasures: Big Joe Williams's *Piney Woods Blues* on the Delmar label, and *Robert Johnson: King of the Delta Blues Singers.* I held the records in literally trembling fingers, pored over the notes in the store, studied the romantic cover painting of an isolated, featureless Robert Johnson hunched over his guitar, paid the $2.89 or so that a record cost then, and took the subway back to Columbia without making any of my other intended stops. I probably listened to each record half a dozen times that day.

Sometimes I can evoke the breathless rush of feeling that I experienced the first time that I ever really heard Robert Johnson's music. Sometimes a note will suggest just a hint of the realms of emotion that opened up to me in that moment, the sense of utter wonder, the shattering revelation. I don't know if it's possible to recreate this kind of feeling today—not because music of similar excitement doesn't exist, but because the discovery can no longer take place in such a void. Or perhaps there is someone right now who will come to Robert Johnson, or a contemporary pop star, or a new voice in jazz, or some music as yet wild and unimagined, with the same sense of innocent expectation that caused my friends and me to hold our breath, all unknowing, when we first played Robert Johnson's songs on the record player. Let me just quote a passage from Rudi Blesh on which an older generation of blues enthusiasts—Mack McCormick, Paul Oliver, probably Sam Charters—was nurtured and which expresses, I think, that same sense of pure romantic surrender. It describes Johnson's masterful "Hell Hound On My Trail" in words that come close to mocking their meaning and yet evoke that same sense of awe I am trying to suggest.

The voice sings and then—on fateful descending notes—echoes its own phrases or imitates the wind, mournfully and far away, in *huh-uh-uh-ummm*, subsiding like a moan on the same ominous, downward cadence. The high, sighing guitar notes vanish sud-

[ 3 ]

denly into silence as if swept away by cold autumn wind. Plangent, iron chords intermittently walk, like heavy footsteps, on the same descending minor series. The images—the wanderer's voice and its echoes, the mocking wind running through the guitar strings, and the implacable, slow, pursuing footsteps—are full of evil, surcharged with the terror of one alone among the moving, unseen shapes of the night. Wildly and terribly, the notes paint a dark wasteland, starless, ululant with bitter wind, swept by the chill rain. Over a hilltop trudges a lonely, ragged, bedeviled figure, bent to the wind, with his *easy rider* held by one arm as it swings from its cord around his neck.

—*Shining Trumpets: A History of Jazz*, 1946

Or, as Greil Marcus wrote, only a little more deliberately, in his 1975 *Mystery Train*: "Johnson's vision was of a world without salvation, redemption or rest. . . . Johnson's music is so strong that in certain moods it can make you feel that he is giving you more than you could have bargained for—that there is a place for you in these lines of his. . . . Johnson's music changed the way the world looked to me."

Revisionist blues historians sometimes suggest that Robert Johnson is derivative, that what seemed so startlingly original has in fact clear antecedents, that Johnson comes from a strong Mississippi Delta tradition which encompassed Charley Patton and Tommy Johnson who, because they came earlier, must have been greater. All of this seems strangely beside the point to me when compared to the unabashedly apocalyptic effect of the music, the still startling and contemporary vision, the selective *artistry* of the work.

Robert Johnson has been a constant presence in my life ever since that first long-playing record—of sides that were originally recorded twenty-five years before that—came out nearly thirty years ago. I can no longer listen as fresh and unencumbered as I once did, obviously, but the music retains *its* freshness, Robert Johnson's music remains the touchstone against which the achievement of the blues is measured.

The album sold ten or twelve thousand copies in its first ten years of existence, and a second volume came out in 1970 which, while it recapitulated Johnson's greatness, didn't really add to it. It completed the *oeuvre*, however; all twenty-nine originals along with three alternate takes were now released. Primarily through the Rolling Stones and Eric Clapton and their versions of Johnson's "Love In Vain" and "Crossroads" in particular, the language of Robert Johnson entered into the common vocabulary of rock. It seems unlikely at this point that there are many people with an interest in contemporary music who are not familiar with one or two of Johnson's tunes—"Dust My Broom," "Sweet Home Chicago," "Stop Breakin' Down," "Walkin' Blues"—even if they are not familiar with their origins.

In addition, new sources of information have sprung up. Johnny Shines, who was himself rediscovered in 1965 and traveled with Johnson for several years in the thirties, has proved a most articulate guide in his recollections of Johnson and in his arresting recreations of Johnson's songs. Even more improbably, Mack McCormick, a Houston folklorist, doggedly pursued the most tenuous leads and over a five-year period in the late sixties and early seventies actually unearthed sisters, widow, children, and photographs of Robert Johnson as well as a death certificate (actually found first by Gayle Dean Wardlow) which fixes the date of death as August 16, 1938, in Greenwood, Mississippi. McCormick has gone a long way toward filling the enormous void of knowledge surrounding Johnson's life and in 1976 announced that he had completed a book, tentatively entitled *Biography of a Phantom* and structured as a mystery, which will undoubtedly add a great deal more to our understanding when it is finally published. The lyrics over which we agonized have long since been thoroughly deciphered, annotated, and analyzed, and seem almost laughably accessible today when one thinks of the hours spent in fruitless speculation.

And yet the essential mystery remains: Who was Robert Johnson? He may well be known to have been born and died on certain dates; his relatives may have vivid memories of him; and his work has long since been placed within a context. Like Shakespeare, though, the man remains the mystery. How was one individual, unschooled and seemingly undifferentiated from his fellows by background or preparation, able to create an *oeuvre* so original, of such sweeping scope and power, however slender the actual body of work may have been in Johnson's case? From what remote and isolated well of inspiration did the music and poetry of Robert Johnson emerge? Answers do not readily suggest themselves. To Mack McCormick Johnson remains "a cipher." To Johnny Shines he was almost "neutral." To his stepson, Robert Jr. Lockwood, a moody, introspective man himself, Robert Johnson was a "loner." For us he may well remain a strange and ultimately inexplicable figure, as driven, as desperate as the subject of Rudi Blesh's description, as foreign still as the

*Johnny Shines, Beloit Blues Festival, 1970.*
DIANE ALLMEN. COURTESY OF LIVING BLUES.

"good-looking boy" described by producer Don Law who "had the most beautiful hands I've ever seen—long, slender fingers," but who Law estimated incorrectly had never been off the plantation.

In the pictures that is one of the things you notice first: his hands. Also his dapper dress, his knowing bow to the camera, his essential inscrutability. Even in the presence of the image, one is left still contemplating the mystery of the man and his music. Had Robert Johnson survived, like Elvis, like his near-contemporary, Howlin' Wolf (actually Wolf was a little older), one wonders if his legend would have been quite so impenetrable. Had he been rediscovered in Chicago living in a project, infirm, alcoholic, vaguely embittered— what would we have made of his legend then? On my desk I have a cotton boll, given to me by Mack McCormick, which is supposedly from the field in Three Forks outside of Greenwood, Mississippi, where Robert Johnson was playing in a little shack when he was murdered. I stare at it, looking like anyone else for significance in an artifact that has no significance. The music has significance. The act of creation was Robert Johnson's statement in a world that lacked consistent purpose or even the sense of cohesiveness, however misleading, that an era of sophisticated communication has supplied. It was a world in which Robert Johnson was suddenly elevated to significance by an act of creative will, by a synthesis of all he knew, of all he ever was to be.

*. . . while Hot Springs' star is still Robert Johnson, who has turned out to be a worker on a Robinsville [sic], Miss. plantation. It is too bad that Vocalion, which is the only company that takes regular trips through the backwoods of the South, records no work songs or songs of protest by Negro artists.*

*—Melody Maker,* July 1937

I T IS EVIDENT by now that Robert Johnson excited an extraordinary amount of interest among blues historians long before the emergence of such a formal study seemed even remotely possible. It was this brief item, published in both England and America during Johnson's lifetime, that fixed the focus of much research—nearly all of it fruitless until Mack McCormick found the unlocking key—around

Robinsonville, at the top of the Mississippi Delta, thirty miles from Memphis. As early as 1939, less than a year after Johnson's death, Alan Lomax, the indefatigable field researcher just then starting out on his career, began his own research on Johnson and his background. Within a couple of years Lomax had discovered Johnson's mentor, Son House, in Lake Cormorant, just north of Robinsonville, on information supplied by McKinley Morganfield (later to become famous as Muddy Waters), another of Johnson's disciples. In fact Lomax and Hammond were talking of a posthumous album of Johnson's recordings at this time, and Mack McCormick started getting letters in Houston in 1948 from European collectors looking for information on Johnson's murder, which was then thought to have taken place in San Antonio, the site of Johnson's first recording session. Robert Johnson may have been the occasion for legend, then, but he was also the subject of intense scrutiny from afar almost from the moment he made his first records. That is what is so ironic about the single factor that obscured the search for Robert Johnson by collectors and other researchers: Robert Johnson, recording star, myth, and legend, was for the most part not known by his own name. He was known as Robert Spencer, R. L. Spencer, occasionally Robert Dodds and, according to Mack McCormick, by a couple of other names— but seldom to family and other intimates as Robert Johnson. It is almost as if Elvis Presley had vanished into the Memphis projects under his mother's maiden name after recording his handful of sides for Sun. It seems particularly ironic that a figure whose achievement set off a virtually global search should have been able to retreat into such total obscurity. But then that, too, is part of the legend.

*Mississippi Delta, June 1937.*
DOROTHEA LANGE. LIBRARY OF CONGRESS, FSA.

Robert Johnson was born probably May 8, 1911, the eleventh child of Julia Major Dodds, whose ten older children were all the offspring of her marriage to Charles Dodds. Robert was illegitimate, which, according to McCormick, was the cause of the name confusion and the cause of many of Johnson's later problems. Charles Dodds and Julia Major married in Hazlehurst, Mississippi, in 1889, when Dodds was twenty-two years old. Dodds, who died in 1940, was a wicker-furniture maker and landowner, and the family was quite well off until Dodds had a falling out with the Marchetti brothers, prominent local landowners, and was forced to leave Hazlehurst around 1909, according to McCormick, with a lynch mob in hot pursuit. Apparently there was a family legend about this escape, which took place with Dodds disguised in women's clothes, and over the next two years Julia managed to send the children one by one to live with their father in Memphis, where he had adopted the name of Spencer. Julia meanwhile stayed on in Hazlehurst with two daughters, Bessie and Carrie, until she was evicted for non-payment of taxes by the intervention of the Marchettis. By this time Robert had been born to Julia and a plantation worker named Noah Johnson, and Julia traveled around from plantation to plantation, living in labor camps, picking cotton, with eight-year-old Carrie taking care of the baby. "Julia spent the next decade trying to reunite the family," says McCormick, "but because of Robert failed. He was the stumbling block. This outside child was very much resented by Charlie Dodds, and though he eventually accepted Robert, he never accepted the mother back."

Through Julia's persistence Charles Dodds Spencer eventually took in Robert around 1914, into a family that now included all of his children by Julia as well as his mistress from Hazlehurst and *their* two children. Robert spent the next few years in Memphis, learned the rudiments of guitar from his brother, Charles Leroy, and was not reunited with his mother until she, remarried now to Willie "Dusty" Willis, reappeared on Front Street. "That's Mama," exclaimed her daughter Carrie, who had not seen their mother for several years. It was at this point, probably around 1918 or 1920, that Robert Leroy Dodds Spencer returned to the Delta, to the area around Robinsonville, where he was brought up by his mother and her husband, Dusty Willis.

Evidently, the confusion—of roles and names—persisted. Robert is said to have taken on the name Johnson as a teenager, when he learned who his real father was, but he didn't get along with his stepfather in any case. "I never heard him talk about any of his people," say Robert Jr. Lockwood and Johnny Shines, "except for his stepfather." According to some recollections, he was known as Little Robert Dusty. According to Son House, who moved to Robinsonville in 1930 after recording for Paramount with Charley Patton and met Johnson, then around nineteen, shortly thereafter: "His mother and stepfather didn't like for him to go out to those Saturday night balls because the guys were so rough. He didn't care anything about working in the fields, and his father was so tight on him about slipping out and coming where we were, so he just got the idea he'd run away from home." McCormick's research bears out the general impression that stepfather and stepson did not exactly see eye to eye. "Robert's stepfather was called Dusty because he would walk so fast he would swirl the dust up all around him. He was a superb farmworker from the boss's point of view, but he had no tolerance of music whatsoever. He was a short stocky man, a real workhorse, and they just had incessant battles."

Robert may or may not have attended school in Commerce, outside of Robinsonville, while he was living on the Abbay and Leatherman Plantation. A number of years ago Johnny Shines, a self-educated man with wide-ranging interests, said of him, "No, Robert didn't have no education at all as far as I could tell. I never saw him read or write, not even his name. He was just a natural genius." More recently it has come out that he was at least able to write some words,

*Plantation owner with field hands, near Clarksdale,*
*Mississippi, 1936.*

DOROTHEA LANGE. LIBRARY OF CONGRESS, FSA.

and Shines himself has expressed the opinion that "Robert had beautiful handwriting. His writing looked like a woman's writing." In any case, according to Shines, he was definitely "anti-education," and it seems clear that music was his first interest. He started out concentrating on jew's harp and harmonica, and by 1930 had married and seriously taken up guitar. His wife died in childbirth at the age of sixteen, and some two months later Son House arrived in Robinsonville.

A word here should probably be said about the direct

line of musical descent commonly perceived in the Mississippi blues tradition. Through the research of David Evans and Gayle Dean Wardlow in particular, the origins of this unique style—generally considered to be the richest and most emotionally intense vein of a genre that began sweeping the South in the early days of the century and then, much assisted by the new technology of the phonograph record, became a central strand in the diffusion of Afro-American culture over the next fifty years—have become clear.

The so-called Delta style of blues singing and playing actually originated around Drew, in the heart of the Delta, around the time that Robert Johnson was born. It centered around a singer named Charley Patton, born in the late 1880s, who was living on Will Dockery's Plantation, between Drew and Boyle, at the time. Willie Brown, a native of Clarksdale, moved to Drew around 1910 and learned from Patton, whose repertoire encompassed knife pieces, church songs, frailed old-time dance numbers, and popular tunes of the day—all sung in a hoarse, impassioned voice not dissimilar to that of another of his students, Howlin' Wolf, who moved to Drew with his family in 1926. Tommy Johnson, too, another of the most influential country bluesmen on record, came to Drew in 1912 and again in 1916 as part of a general migration from the Crystal Springs area south of Jackson. Johnson returned to Crystal Springs for good in the early 1920s with his lyrical adaptation of Patton's style, and his first records included snatches from Patton's showpiece, "Hitch Up My Pony, Saddle Up My Black Mare," the first song that Howlin' Wolf ever played on the guitar. Willie Brown moved up to the Robinsonville area in 1926, and Howlin' Wolf followed suit in the thirties. Son House, a keen student of Patton's, with a fervent, deep voice, was taken by his mentor to Charley's fourth recording session for the Paramount Record Company, which took place on May 28, 1930, in Grafton, Wisconsin. For the session Patton also brought along pianist Louise Johnson and his former partner, Willie Brown, by then living in Robinsonville. After the session was over—an historic documentation of four major artists—House returned to Lula briefly, then moved to Robinsonville, where he and Willie Brown formed a musical partnership that was to last over the next twenty years. This was the musical legacy that Robert Johnson inherited, and I have gone into it at such length only to show the actual way in which it appears to have been transmitted.

"We'd all play for the Saturday night balls," Son House told folklorist Julius Lester, "and there'd be this little boy standing around. That was Robert Johnson. He was just a little boy then. He blew a harmonica and he was pretty good with that, but he wanted to play a guitar. When we'd leave at night to go play for the balls, he'd slip off and come over to where we were. . . . He'd get where Willie and I were and sit right down on the floor and watch from one to the other. And when we'd get a break and want to rest some, we'd set the guitars up in the corner and go out in the cool. Robert would watch and see which way we'd gone, and he would pick one of them up. And such another racket you never heard! It'd make the people mad, you know. They'd come out and say, 'Why don't y'all go in and get that guitar away from that boy! He's running people crazy with it.' I'd come back in, and I'd scold him about it. 'Don't do that, Robert. You drive the people nuts. You can't play nothing. Why don't you blow the harmonica for 'em?' But he didn't want to blow that. Still, he didn't care how I'd get after him about it. He'd do it anyway."

It's hard to reconcile the dates in the various accounts. By House's chronology the "little boy" that he remembers must have been nineteen or twenty years old, already married, and a widower. We know that while he was married he lived with his sister Bessie and her husband, Granville Hines, in Penton, close to Robinsonville. Evidently, if Son House's account is to be believed, he then moved back in with his mother and her husband but found the same conflicts that he had experienced all through childhood. He left home once again but this time went deep into the Delta and

*Jitterbugging on a Saturday afternoon, Clarksdale, 1939.*
MARION POST WOLCOTT. LIBRARY OF CONGRESS, FSA.

married for a second time, in 1931, near his birthplace of Hazlehurst, about forty miles south of Jackson, not far from Tommy Johnson's home base of Crystal Springs. For the next year or so he traveled all through the Delta, using Hazlehurst as a base. When he returned, Son House and Willie Brown had a surprise coming.

"Willie and I were playing again out at a little place east of Robinsonville called Banks, Mississippi. We were playing there one Saturday night, and all of a sudden somebody came in through the door. Who but him! He had a guitar swinging on his back. I said, 'Bill!' He said, 'Huh?' I said, 'Look who's coming in the door.' He looked and said, 'Yeah. Little Robert.' I said, 'And he's got a guitar.' And Willie and I laughed about it. Robert finally wiggled through the crowd and got to where we were. He spoke, and I said, 'Well, boy, you still got a guitar, huh? What do you do with that thing? You can't do nothing with it.' He said, 'Well, I'll tell you what.' I said, 'What?' He said, 'Let me have your seat a minute.' So I said, 'All right, and you better do something with it, too,' and I winked my eye at Willie. So he sat down there and finally got started. And man! He was so good! When he finished, all our mouths were standing open. I said, 'Well, ain't that fast! He's gone now!'"

Many stories have been advanced to account for such sudden proficiency in the blues, and probably all of them have been told about Robert. As Johnny Shines has said about his own superstitious awe of Howlin' Wolf, "People back then thought about magic and all such things as that. I didn't know it at the time, but Wolf was a tractor driver. As far as I knew, he could have crawled out of a cave, a place of solitude, after a full week's rest, to serenade us. I thought he was a magic man, he looked different than anyone I'd seen, and I come along and say a guy that played like Wolf, he'd sold his soul to the devil."

Tommy Johnson's brother LeDell put it to David Evans even more graphically in describing how Tommy, who like Robert went off from home scarcely able to play the guitar, came back an accomplished musician.

> Now if Tom was living, he'd tell you. He said the reason he knowed so much, said he sold hisself to the devil. I asked him how. He said, "If you want to learn how to play anything you want to play and learn how to make songs yourself, you take your guitar and you go to where a road crosses that way, where a crossroad is. Get there, be sure to get there just a little 'fore 12:00 that night so you'll know you'll be there. You have your guitar and be playing a piece there by yourself. . . . A big black man will walk up there and take your guitar, and he'll tune it. And then he'll play a piece and hand it back to you. That's the way I learned to play anything I want."

Son House was convinced that Robert Johnson had done the same thing, and undoubtedly, as Johnny Shines says, others were, too. That was the beginning, in any case, of Robert Johnson's travels and of his life as a professional musician. He stayed around, in House's recollection, about a week. Then, using Helena, Memphis, Greenwood, in addition to Robinsonville, as his base, Johnson traveled all up and down the Delta and, as he gained greater fame, to St.

Louis, Chicago, Detroit, and New York as well. He came to know a good number of professional musicians—Robert Nighthawk and Sonny Boy Williamson in Helena, Henry Townsend, Peetie Wheatstraw, Roosevelt Sykes in St. Louis—and gained a considerable reputation for himself in the process. When Johnny Shines first met him in Helena in the mid-thirties, Shines was taken there by a friend, a piano player named M&O, who "wanted me to meet Robert, because this friend of mine thought I were good. You know how this thing goes. There's a good guy playing at such and such a place, I'd like for you to meet him. And the thing about it, what he wants you to do is to go and get your head cut. So M&O finally talked me into going to see him, and Robert played a good guitar, the best I'd heard. Now I had Wolf's style in the beginning, and I was beginning to pick up on quite a few different guys' styles as the time went along, but I thought Robert was about the greatest guitar player I'd ever heard. The things he was doing was things that I'd never heard nobody else do, and I wanted to learn it. Robert changed everything, what you might say."

Henry Townsend, a professional musician living in St. Louis who had made recordings as early as 1929, was no less impressed. He met Robert at a house-rent party on Jefferson Avenue, had never heard of him, "his name didn't mean anything to me. . . . But to me he was such a good musician! I thought he was great; matter of fact, my ambition was to keep in touch with him as much as I could, because, to me, he was a rare type of executor of music."

Evidently Johnson had the entertainer's gift of establishing an almost instant rapport with his audience as well as with his peers. "Some people have it and some people don't," says Johnny Shines. "Now, you take that some musicians is great artists, but they don't take with the public like others. Well, Robert was one of those fellows who was warm in every respect—in *every* respect. Even, you know, it's natural for men not to like a musician too much. But Robert was a fellow very well liked by women and men, even though a lot of men resented his power or his influence over woman-people. They resented that very much, but, as a human being, they still liked him because they couldn't help but like him, for Robert just had that power to draw."

Everywhere he went he was hailed and remembered—in Arkansas and Mississippi, hill country and Delta, city and town. He traveled by bus and by train, hitching a ride on the back of a pickup truck, sitting in the back of a corn wagon with a tractor pulling it. Sometimes he and a companion like Johnny Shines would set off walking down the highway; other times they would hop a train pulling out of the freight yards. When they arrived in a new town they would play on street corners or in front of the local barbershop, set up in front of restaurants or in the town square, reestablish some local connection to make a house-rent party in the city or a house-rocking get-back at some plantation shack out from town. To drum up additional interest, Robert sometimes described himself as "one of the Johnson boys"—referring to recording stars Lonnie and Tommy—and would occasionally claim that his initials R. L. stood for Robert Lonnie. Johnny Shines describes arriving in a strange town, not knowing anyone, covered with the dirt and grime of the road. "But Robert was always neat. Robert could ride highways and things like that all day long, and you'd look down at yourself and you'd be as filthy as a pig and Robert'd be

*Vicksburg, Mississippi, March 1936.*
WALKER EVANS. LIBRARY OF CONGRESS, FSA.

clean—how, I don't know. In those days you didn't have to
know nowhere to go. People would just pick you up on the
streets—they'd see you with your instrument, say, 'Man, you
play that?' 'Yeah.' 'Play me a piece.' You say, 'Well, I do this
for my living, man,' and by that they know automatically
you're not going to be playing for free. Maybe you stand there
and play two or three pieces—well, by that time, hell, you
got twenty-five or thirty people around you."

You had to be prepared to play what your audience
wanted you to play, since you were being paid not by salary
but by tips. You might be engaged to play all night at a juke

joint for a dollar and a half, but you were liable to make your real money by filling a request for Leroy Carr's latest release or a Duke Ellington number. By Johnny Shines's account Robert Johnson was as likely to perform "Tumbling Tumbleweeds" or the latest Bing Crosby hit as one of his own compositions. "You didn't play what *you* liked; you played what the people liked. That's what you had to do." By Shines's and just about everyone else's account, Johnson possessed a singular facility not only for discovering what the people liked but for learning a tune simply by hearing it once on the radio or jukebox. "Robert could play anything. He could play in the style of Lonnie Johnson, Blind Blake, Blind Boy Fuller, Blind Willie McTell, all those guys. And the country singer—Jimmie Rodgers—me and Robert used to play a hell of a lot of his tunes, man. Ragtime, pop tunes, waltz numbers, polkas—shoot, a polka hound, man. Robert just picked songs out of the air. You could have the radio on, and he'd be talking to you and you'd have no idea that he'd be thinking about it because he'd go right on talking, but later he'd play that song note for note. Hillbilly, blues, and all the rest."

It's a little hard to imagine what an actual performance must have sounded like. According to Shines and Robert Lockwood people listened more to the words in those days because "they had reason to listen to the words, they was *living* the words." On the other hand, no great distinction was made between popular and original material, and evidently no great distinction was made in genres either. It is perhaps easier to envision Robert Johnson singing "My Blue Heaven" to a crowd in town on market day than it is to imagine the effect that "Hell Hound On My Trail," one of his bleakest and most terrifying songs, would have on this same crowd, black or white. Unquestionably, he sang songs like "Come On In My Kitchen" and "Terraplane," his signature piece once he started recording, because both had a sly sense of double entendre that would have been as popular in the thirties as it is today. At a dance, undoubtedly he concentrated on his strongest rhythmic pieces. Johnny Shines has said that those who wanted to hear the lyrics would gather around the singer at the front, and he and Lockwood also contend that sound carried so much further in the country, without the background distractions of traffic or airplanes, that even at a crowded dance people were more attentive to nuance. Nonetheless, I think the description that Shines gave to Pete Welding of a typical country getback is even more evocative of the spirit of the occasion. "Robert sang pretty loud, and most of the time he sang in a high-pitched voice, and, naturally, his voice was carrying. We didn't have too much trouble in having ourselves heard in those places we played in. The people that was dancing, they'd just pick up the beat, and if they got out of earshot, I guess the rhythm just stayed with them and they kept right on dancing. Because the whole house had the same motion. . . ."

Like anyone for whom the road becomes home, Robert Johnson established safe harbors everywhere he went, links within the community which he could put down and pick up again when he returned in a month or a year. In Helena he established a relationship with Robert Jr. Lockwood's mother, probably fifteen years older than he, which was evidently as stable over a long period of time as any on which he embarked. Robert Jr. Lockwood, who went on to become one of the most progressive-minded of Chicago bluesmen and a stalwart session musician for Chess Records (he was named Jr. for his father but continues to be called so for his connection with Robert Johnson), recalls Johnson with a respect that borders on reverence, though he was only three or four years younger than his stepfather. He wanted to be a piano player until he met Johnson, probably when he was around seventeen or eighteen years old, and speaks fondly of how his stepfather helped him make his second guitar from the back of a record player with hay baling wire for frets.

Johnny Shines first met Lockwood through Robert Johnson when the two younger men were nineteen or twenty years old, and he says that of all Johnson's relationships, the most durable were the ones with Robert Lockwood's mother and Walter Horton's sister. But even these were merely stops along the way. In West Memphis Johnson and Shines and Shines's cousin, Calvin Frazier, stayed at the Hunt Hotel, where Robert took up with a female midget who ran errands for the three bluesmen. In Friars Point there was a "runty little girl named Betty." In every town in which they stopped there was someone to take care of Johnson, a woman—not necessarily a "glamour girl," but someone who would look after him. "Women, to Robert," Shines has written, "were like motel or hotel rooms: even if he used them repeatedly he left them where he found them." Nor was his predilection for older women difficult to understand. "Heaven help him, he was not discriminating. Probably a bit like Christ, he loved them all. He preferred older women in their thirties over the younger ones, because the older ones would pay his way." Mack McCormick discovered at least half a dozen women involved in two- or three-week relationships in the eight years following his first wife's death. By McCormick's account they were shy young girls for the most part, similar to the older women whom Shines describes in one respect: they provided food and shelter for a footloose musician and were not considered the most desirable or attractive catches in the community. "Johnson had a very unusual reputation. He was not crude, but he was direct. Almost all the women describe him as shy; they describe his first words as a blunt statement put in a shy way. He would simply ask them: 'Can I go home with you? Can I be with you?' These were young girls living with their families in a rural situation, and for the most part their answer was yes. The relationship ended when their husbands came home or Johnson moved on."

Probably too much has been made of Johnson's sexual magnetism, of the very exoticness of his life. Johnny Shines and Robert Lockwood saw Johnson as somewhat immature and lacking in common sense or judgment. "Robert would do some funny things," says Robert Jr., "that I didn't like. Things would just create around him, and I always tried to stay out of trouble, so I just decided I wouldn't be with him no more." Shines has described the hypnotic effect of his music, and there is no question that a song like "Come On In My Kitchen" was an open invitation to get to know the singer better. But then so are most blues, and so is most rock 'n' roll as well. The thing most commonly misunderstood is just how shadowy was the world in which Robert Johnson was moving about.

It was the mid-1930s, to be sure; cars were traveling on the highways; Robert Johnson's sister had a telephone in Penton, and another sister owned a juke joint with a "piccolo" (jukebox) in Bunker Hill in Memphis. Howlin' Wolf started playing with an electric guitar some time around this period on the streets of Drew, and in just a few years a friend of B. B. King's would bring him home Django Reinhardt records from Europe in the aftermath of the Second World War. Johnny Shines, whose education was interrupted in about the sixth grade, took night courses after he moved to Chicago, and even when he was traveling with Johnson, he says, read by the light of a streetlamp when they stayed at a rooming house or private home in town.

But all these modernities notwithstanding, communication in the world in which Robert Johnson lived was almost exclusively oral, and although contacts were made and tales were told, the contacts were almost always tangential; the stories—while often maintaining a basis in fact—were in a sense as mythopoetic as those of the ancient Greeks. Johnny Shines and Robert Lockwood, playing partners today, met, for example, through Johnson and became friendly years later in Chicago, but though each was well aware of the other, neither shares a single experience or memory of their time with Johnson. In a certain sense, in fact, each is suspicious of the other's memories and of the memories of others, because in their experience *it simply didn't happen that way.* Shines remembers an illiterate Robert Johnson, and Lockwood scoffs at the suggestion, which in turn seems to prompt a shift in Shines's memory. Howlin' Wolf, who admired Johnson enormously, knew nothing of his family, and Lockwood knew nothing of his influences, because, as each quite candidly admits, "I didn't care nothing about that." Even Johnny Shines, who was as close to Robert as any of his playing partners and recalls him with a vividness that is altogether convincing, insists, "I didn't know he had relatives

*Robert Jr. Lockwood and Sonny Boy Williamson
(Rice Miller), early 1940s.*

MAX MOORE. COURTESY OF MIKE ROWE / BLUES UNLIMITED.

in Memphis, he never mentioned his people. So many things I found out later I didn't know at the time, because I just wasn't interested."

Of all the stories that are told of Robert Johnson, I think one of Robert Lockwood's best illustrates the anomalousness of the world in which he lived, the compartmentalization that necessarily existed before radio—let alone television—let in the world outside.

"I went down to Elaine, Arkansas, one time," says Lockwood matter-of-factly, "looking for myself. That's right. I was down in Elaine playing one night, and the next day I came back home and here come a dude meet me, say, 'Hey, man, Robert Johnson is down in Elaine. Yeah. I went down and stood and looked at him play, man.' Well, I hadn't seen Robert in a long time, and I turned right around and I went back to Elaine, and it wasn't until I got back down there that I realized that man done come and looked at me playing and got me going back down there looking for myself!"

Within this welter of confusion, of parallel lines that never meet or like railroad tracks might come to a crossing at a switching point like Helena, say, and then continue on their independent ways, Robert Johnson seems always to have sought to make connections, to have hungered—despite his solitary nature, or perhaps because of it—for some form of companionship. Robert Lockwood's touchstone was his mother. Johnny Shines's family was centered in Memphis and Arkansas. Johnson, because of his fragmented and complicated family history, had farflung connections all through the Delta and into Tennessee. According to Mack McCormick, these were what he always came back to, something like twenty households scattered throughout a number of plantations as well as the homes of Charlie Dodds and his sisters in Memphis. "Many of these people didn't know each other, though he stayed initially in the web of the families: Charlie Dodds, Dodds's stepchildren, Julia, Julia's ten or twelve uncles, his brothers and sisters and acquaintances. His life was divided into any number of networks or compartments, each of which was discrete, each of which knew him by different names."

Throughout all of them he moved as a solitary figure, cryptic, guarded, somewhat secretive, in McCormick's words a little bit of a cipher. If you asked someone who hadn't seen him in a long time to describe a bluesman like Johnny Shines, say, or Robert Lockwood, or Howlin' Wolf, vivid descriptions would be forthcoming, adjectives would come pouring out. Each of these musicians makes a definite impression, even if, as in the case of Lockwood, it is that he is aloof, standoffish, somewhat removed. With Robert Johnson the words are all abstract. He was "polite." He was "shy." He was "the nicest guy in the world," an "awful friendly guy," "a little moody," "childish," "kind of reckless." He was always neat. He didn't like to play with anyone else much, and no one who traveled with him ever considered himself a partner. He was well-mannered, he was soft-spoken, he was indecipherable. No one seems to have any idea where the music came from.

But then it was a world in which everyone was chasing shadows. How could the teenage Chester Burnett (Howlin' Wolf) ever have imagined that he would one day become an international celebrity when he was picking cotton in Drew, Mississippi, and learning how to play "Saddle My Pony" from a local roustabout named Charley Patton? How could Muddy Waters, married at sixteen in Stovall, Mississippi, ever dream that he would be featured in the pages of a magazine like *Rolling Stone*, named, like the group, for a song that probably everyone in the Delta sang at one time or another and that he recorded in 1950 for a big r & b hit? There were no goals. There were no ends. Muddy Waters, Johnny Shines, Robert Lockwood, Howlin' Wolf, and Robert Johnson were bright, imaginative young men who knew what they *didn't* want, which was to pick cotton like their parents or be stuck in a rural backwater where their music was a diversion—but a diversion only—from backbreaking labor.

*Lunchtime for cotton hoers, near Clarksdale, 1937.*
DOROTHEA LANGE. LIBRARY OF CONGRESS, FSA.

Education was not available; perspective was not possible; there was little family or economic stability. The world in which they lived was enshrouded by fog but enlivened by their music and a sense of expectation and adventure, of having to create around them the coherence and connections that were otherwise lacking in their lives. "Sometimes we had money," says Johnny Shines, who has often described the life in almost poetic terms, "sometimes we didn't. Sometimes we had food, sometimes we had some place to stay, sometimes we didn't. Well, it's very exciting. Say for an instance you leave here, you maybe go four or five hundred miles, and you don't know anybody, everything is new to you. See, Robert was a guy, you could wake him up anytime and he was ready to *go*. Say, for instance, you had come from Memphis and go to Helena, and we'd play there all night probably and lay down to sleep the next morning, and you hear a train. You say, 'Robert, I hear a train; let's catch it.' He wouldn't exchange no words with you; he's just ready to go. It's really, I mean if a person lives in an exploratory world, then this is the best thing that ever happened to him."

Probably this kind of nomadic life could have gone on indefinitely, with any number of predictable variations. Robert might have moved to Chicago like Shines, settled down and gotten a day job, or become a star like Muddy Waters and Howlin' Wolf after the war. He might have continued, like Elmore James, Big Joe Williams, or Robert Nighthawk, traversing the Delta, heading for Florida when the crops came in, returning to Texas, Detroit, Oklahoma, constantly visiting—as Big Joe put it—"the four corners of the world," from California to Bangor, Maine. He might have survived, like Big Joe, into the folk and blues revival of the sixties, which carried bluesmen even beyond the four corners of the world, to Europe and Japan. He might, as Johnny Shines and Robert Lockwood suggest, have taken up jazz stylings which would have been unlikely to add to his popularity with the public but could well have increased his reputation as a musician's musician. He might have given up blues altogether, his pact with the devil at an end, or died the same death that he did, poisoned at a little country crossroads by the husband of a woman he had been seeing, without anyone ever having known of him or his work except those who had actually heard him sing and play. Then his legend would have taken on even additional stature perhaps; he would be known as the missing link between Son House and Muddy Waters, a man of many names, whose stylistic inventiveness could only be imagined. There is no telling what would have happened to Robert Johnson, because there is no real distinguishing of him from his contemporaries except for one factor, the most important factor from history's point of view (is there anything that can truly be said to exist without documentation?): his recordings.

Robert Johnson recorded, not entirely coincidentally, through the same man who brought Charley Patton, Son House, Skip James, the Mississippi Sheiks, Tommy Johnson, and nearly every other Mississippi blues singer of any consequence into the recording studio. H. C. Speir, a white man, ran a music store in Jackson and got into business as a talent scout initially to assure himself of a good supply of records to sell. He claimed, in interviews with David Evans and Gayle Dean Wardlow, never to care for any one form of music in particular, but his taste in blues seems to have been impeccable, and his influence on American music in this mode is virtually without parallel, save for Sam Phillips's decade at Sun and the Chess brothers' sway at Chess Records. Skip James has described what must have been a typical audition session: the singers lined up in Speir's record store, all the best performers from miles around gathered together by notices in the paper and word of mouth. All got an audition; some were cut off after only one or two verses; Skip himself was the only one to pass at his particular tryout, after singing no more than two verses from his signature piece, "Devil Got My Woman."

Robert Johnson came into Speir's store some time in 1936, when he was twenty-four or twenty-five years old. Obviously Speir's reputation by this time, nearly seven years after Patton's first recordings, had solidified in the black community; the number of singers whom he had brought to a recording contract was well known; his influence with the record companies was evident; and his store was undoubtedly a hangout for all kinds of aspiring musicians, where records (acetates for demo purposes) were actually cut. When Johnson came in to see him, Speir was working for the ARC label group, for whom he had recorded nearly two hundred sides in Jackson and Hattiesburg. Of these, only forty had been issued, so Speir passed the name of the young man on to Ernie Oertle, who was a talent scout and salesman for ARC in the mid-South. Oertle heard Johnson and offered to take him to San Antonio to record in November of 1936.

Johnson must have been elated. To someone like Son House, who remained a local musician primarily, recording was a memorable experience, but as much for the exoticness of the setting and the income the few sides provided as for the potential to become more widely popular or even to be remembered by posterity. Such considerations probably didn't even come into play. For a self-conceived professional musician like Skip James or Robert Johnson, however, recording must have offered the opportunity to make a statement; it was a validation in its own terms. Robert came into his sister

Carrie's house on Georgia Street jubilant, according to Mack McCormick. "I'm going to Texas to make records," he announced to her, and spoke to other bluesmen with similar pride about his upcoming session. McCormick, whose father was a traveling salesman, like Oertle, in the Depression, retraced Oertle's route to San Antonio and actually found people who still remembered a white man and a black musician passing through. It was a leisurely trip, as Oertle had stops to make and records to sell, and in several communities along the way Oertle had to find Johnson a private home in which to lodge. In Taft, Oklahoma, an all-black community, McCormick found someone who identified Johnson by the song "Terraplane Blues," as yet unrecorded but Johnson's signature piece, which the man was surprised to find out some thirty-five years later had actually come out on record. Johnson was, by this informant's account, an unknown— private, reserved, seemingly inexperienced. Even in outline it seems a peculiar, symbolic odyssey, and it makes up a substantial part of McCormick's projected book.

They arrived in San Antonio in late November, and Oertle brought Johnson over to the Gunter Hotel, where ARC recording director Art Satherley was conducting sessions. He had already been in San Antonio for several weeks and would move on next to Dallas and Fort Worth. The Chuck Wagon Gang, a popular Western Swing band, was recorded on the same days as Johnson, as well as two groups of Mexican musicians led by Andres Berlanga and Francisco Montalvo and Hermanas Barzaza. Don Law, the A&R man in charge of the session, recalled Johnson twenty-five years later on the occasion of the release of the first epochal collection of his recordings, as "a little above medium height,

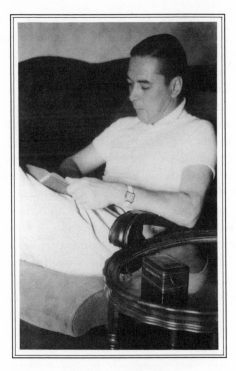

*Don Law, ca. 1930.*
COURTESY OF THE LAW FAMILY.

not real jet black but real black." He was, Law thought, no more than seventeen or eighteen years old, and extremely shy. Law asked Johnson to play guitar for the Mexican musicians in the studio, and "suffering from a bad case of stage fright, Johnson turned his back to the wall, his back to the Mexican musicians. Eventually he calmed down sufficiently to play, but he never faced his audience." This fits in actually with Johnny Shines's and Robert Lockwood's accounts of Johnson as being extremely jealous of his own abilities, turning away from other musicians if he felt their eyes upon him, as if—and again this would bear out the devil theory, which Johnson himself may well have believed, as Tommy Johnson evidently did—he had some dark secret to hide.

In any case Johnson recorded sixteen sides in the three-day session that started on Monday, November 23, and ended Friday, November 27 (Tuesday and Wednesday were skipped; perhaps this gap is explained by Law's famous story of bailing Johnson out of jail on a vagrancy charge, only to have him phone again a few hours later with the complaint, "'I'm lonesome.' Puzzled, Law said, 'You're lonesome? What do you mean, you're lonesome?' Johnson replied, 'I'm lonesome and there's a lady here. She wants fifty cents and I lacks a nickel. . . .'"). If he had never recorded again, his name would have been forever etched in the history of American song.

Of the sixteen selections, three remained unissued altogether until the release of the Columbia albums, along with several of the most emotionally expressive alternate takes. One raucous ragtime number, evidently learned from a brother, was perhaps not uncharacteristic of Johnson's live repertoire but unique within the canon of his recorded work. Several were fairly overt double entendres: "Kind Hearted Woman," the first number cut, was obviously derived from the popular piano player Leroy Carr, though no less distinctive for its ancestry. "I Believe I'll Dust My Broom" and "Sweet Home Chicago" (based on Kokomo Arnold's "Old Original Kokomo Blues") became postwar standards, known to virtually every blues musician, and Johnson's walking bass style on guitar, adapted from boogie woogie piano, while it may not have been entirely original with him, popularized a mode which would rapidly become the accepted pattern. As Johnny Shines has said, "Some of the things that Robert did with the guitar affected the way everybody played. In the early thirties, boogie was rare on the guitar, something to be heard. Because of Robert, people learned to complement theirselves, carrying their own bass as well as their own lead with this one instrument." One song, "Terraplane Blues," was a modest hit; perhaps it sold four or five thousand copies, and became the number for which Johnson is best remembered even today by his contemporaries. Overall, though, it is the breadth and scope and passion of his performance, the tight, somewhat constricted voice breaking occasionally or descending into a not-quite-convincing growl, the guitar perfectly mirroring the vocals, the plangent slide-playing that Johnny Shines said "caused many a woman to weep, and many a man, too," which rivet the attention and force us to focus on the altogether arresting lyrics.

Songs like "Cross Road Blues," "Come On In My Kitchen," the Son House-influenced "Walkin' Blues" and "Preachin' Blues (Up Jumped the Devil)," while certainly not the pinnacle of Johnson's achievement, took the blues into new artistic areas in a new, self-consciously artistic mode. Where someone like Son House or Charley Patton was content to throw together a collection of relatively traditional lyrics, known as "floating verses," which, however effective their emotional impact or even their story-telling specifics, never fully achieved thematic coherence, Johnson intentionally developed themes in his songs; each song made a statement, both metaphorical and real. If he sang plaintively,

"When you got a good friend, have her stick right by your side," that plaintiveness was carried out by guitar and vocal parts throughout the song; "Ramblin' On My Mind" described in actual and poetic terms a consciously considered nomadic life, with the music specifically echoing the theme; a song like "Cross Road Blues," with its immediate evocation both of the devil's bargain and the common dilemma of choice, works on both a very real and a highly metaphorical level, starting off with the statement, "I was standing at the crossroads, I tried to flag a ride / Nobody seemed to know me, everybody passed me by," and concluding: "I'm standing at the crossroads, I believe I'm sinking down." There is no end of quoting and no end of reading into the lyrics, but unlike other equally eloquent blues, this is not random folk art, hit or miss, but rather carefully selected and honed detail, carefully considered and achieved effect. When Johnson asks, "Can't you hear that wind howling?" in "Come On In My Kitchen," both guitar and voice moan with a sexual fall. When he sings on a later session, "I have a bird to whistle, and I have a bird to sing / I've got a woman that I'm loving, but she don't mean a thing," the rightness of the image, the *implicit* connection, recalls without strain Catullus, Gerard Manley Hopkins, John Donne.

Two takes of virtually every number were recorded, with the second meant to be a safety take (in case the master was damaged) and intended to come as close as possible to the first in time, mood, and feeling. In most cases Johnson's first takes are superior, understandably so, though undoubtedly there were false starts and partial takes that preceded these. The drapes of the round top windows in the mezzanine floor of the Gunter Hotel were closed to keep out the noise of traffic, though this was nowhere near as pressing a problem as in busy downtown Dallas, where the second set of recordings would take place six months later. The session wound up with "If I Had Possession Over Judgment Day," a frenziedly emotional performance in the Son House vein based on the familiar "Rollin' and Tumblin'" melodic theme. Perhaps too frankly unrestrained for the ARC catalogue ("If I had possession over judgment day, then the woman that I'm loving wouldn't have no right to pray"), it was not released until the *King of the Delta Blues Singers* album came out in 1961. Robert Johnson finished up the session and headed for home, possibly using the train ticket provided by Ernie Oertle or more likely cashing it in and hopping a freight. He returned home with several hundred dollars in his pocket, undoubtedly more than he had ever seen in his life before. "In my mind he was a nice little quiet-spoken colored boy," said Vince Liebler, the recording engineer for the session.

*We heard a couple of his pieces come out on records. Believe the first one I heard was "Terraplane Blues." Jesus, it was good! We all admired it. Said, "That boy is really going places."*
—SON HOUSE

THERE IS NO QUESTION of the impact that recording made on Robert Johnson's life. Certainly his contemporaries made the distinction, for the jukebox was by now after all a primary source of material and Robert Johnson was a recording star. "Nearly every time I came upon Robert," says Johnny Shines, probably without exaggeration, "he'd be telling me about some new recording session. He'd tell me about things I'd never seen, like 'start lights' and 'stop lights' used in recording. About seventy-five to a hundred dollars was all the money he ever got." Mack McCormick tells of how, when the first records came out, Robert went around to his relatives and his children by various women to bring them the record himself. It makes a curious picture—the neat, always impeccable bluesman walking down a dusty road, shoulders high and hunched a little bit forward, his guitar in one hand, his latest record in the other. Even his father, Noah, with whom there had evidently been very little contact, came to see his son at this point, and there is no question that Robert traveled even more widely but retained his habit of disappearing at a moment's notice ("See, he was a kind of peculiar fellow. Robert'd be standing up playing some place, you know, just playing like nobody's business, but [then] Robert'd just pick up and walk off and leave you standing there playing. And you wouldn't see Robert no more maybe in two or three weeks.") and more than a hint of his reckless ways.

He was called back to record in June 1937, this time in Dallas in a warehouse in the business district (perhaps the upstairs of a Buick showroom) on a Saturday and Sunday when the noise of traffic would not intrude so much. His recording this time was sandwiched in between the Crystal City Ramblers and Zeke Williams and His Rambling Cowboys; he made three masters on the first day and ten on Sunday evening, of which eleven would be released within the next year. It was stifling inside the studio, which led to makeshift attempts at air-conditioning. Don Law described another session of the time in this manner. "To keep the street noises out, we had to keep the windows closed, so we

*Near Port Gibson, Mississippi, August 1940.*
MARION POST WOLCOTT. LIBRARY OF CONGRESS, FSA.

worked shirtless with electric fans blowing across cakes of ice." Safety takes were probably done on most of the numbers, though only four survive, and in each case the alternate is virtually identical to the original. As country star Roy Acuff said of his own first recording session: "By the time you went through the number, timed it out, and then did another number exactly like it—failed on three or four of them—you were simply wore out. . . ." Undoubtedly the same circumstances applied on Robert Johnson's session, but if his enthusiasm waned, there is no evidence of that on the recordings themselves.

The recordings that Robert Johnson made at his second session were, if anything, superior even to the first. Actually, these last dates included both his most inspired and his most derivative recordings. "Malted Milk" and "Drunken Hearted Man" were blatant imitations of Lonnie Johnson, then at the height of his popularity, and while they are professional enough, they only bear out Johnny Shines's contention that Johnson really idolized his more famous namesake. "Honeymoon Blues" is a rather slight, sentimental number, "Little Queen of Spades" fastens on to a tired blues metaphor, and even "Love In Vain"—perhaps Robert Johnson's most familiar legacy to the rock age—is a less than startling takeoff on a Leroy Carr/Big Bill Broonzy theme. There are, in addition, some of his most lovely and most traditional songs. "From Four Until Late" is based on the old "Four O'Clock" blues melody; "Stop Breakin' Down" (also recorded by the Rolling Stones) and "I'm A Steady Rollin' Man," while not extraordinary original compositions, have become staples on the Chicago blues scene. "Traveling Riverside Blues" is out of the "Rollin' and Tumblin'" family, with a twist that kept it from being released at the time ("You can squeeze my lemon," Johnson sang, in a line that thrilled later generations, "till the juice run down my leg"), and "Milkcow's Calf Blues" sounds a little like a cross between Kokomo Arnold and Son

House, on top of a "Terraplane"-like melody. "Stones In My Passway," "Me And The Devil," and "Hell Hound On My Trail," however, are the cornerstones upon which Robert Johnson's posthumous reputation is based.

"Stones In My Passway," like many of his most effective songs, is played with a slide, with the guitar tuned in "Spanish" (open G) and the strings echoing the words almost as a second voice. Also, like a good many of Johnson's most ambitious compositions, it suggests both in its imagery and its language almost Biblical overtones (readily available through popular gospel recordings and preaching) which raise again the whole conflicted nature of Johnson's life and work. And, of course, like the rest of his most emotionally expressive blues, the song suggests levels of real and metaphorical experience that can be extended indefinitely by the imagination of the listener, as he declares: "I got stones in my passway, and my road seems dark as night / I have pains in my heart, they have taken my appetite . . .

> My enemies have betrayed me,
> have overtaken poor Bob at last
> And there's one thing certain,
> they have stones all in my path.

This sense of betrayal is made even more explicit in "Me And The Devil Blues" as Johnson raises the very questions that have been lurking in the background all along: the connection between pleasure and pain, the conflict between the satisfaction of music and its essentially sinful nature, the debt that must be paid for art and the Faustian bargain that Johnson sees at its core.

Early this morning,
　　　when you knocked upon my door
And I said "Hello, Satan,
　　　I believe it's time to go."

Seldom has a number of such direct emotional impact been recorded, but then this is what the blues is supposed to be about. If you listen to Son House, if you listen to Charley Patton or Howlin' Wolf, you hear the same emotional involvement. What is almost breathtaking here is not simply the feeling but the artistry, an artistry not surprising in the tortuous poetry of Gerard Manley Hopkins but virtually unique in the annals of the blues.

That is why it seems altogether appropriate that "Hell Hound On My Trail," Johnson's crowning achievement and one that is almost universally recognized as the apogee of the blues, should have derived melodically from the "Devil Got My Woman" of Skip James, another blues singer of consciously artistic achievement, whose "22-20" Johnson had earlier adapted as his own "32-20" and whose "Four O'Clock Blues" he had also obviously listened to. James was by no means a widely popular musician; he made fewer than twenty known prewar recordings, and none of them sold to the extent that Robert Johnson's did, but they were among the most finely crafted, deliberate, and *odd* recordings made in the history of American popular music. For "Hell Hound On My Trail" (whose title, it has been suggested, stems from Francis Thompson's "Hound of Heaven" and bears in any case clear Biblical associations), Johnson employed James's unique open-E tuning for the only time on record. The lyrics match and sum up the eeriness of the accompaniment, which follows an emotional pattern that no other blues singer that I know of has attempted to reproduce. Thus, although the song is Johnson's crowning achievement, virtually no attempts to cover it have been made. Even putting down the words on paper scarcely suggests the stark terror of the song, and no matter how many times I have listened to it, it still seems to come out of a void, it seems impossible to imagine a recording engineer saying, "Could we have another take of that one, Bob?" though indeed there must have been one (even if none has survived).

> I got to keep movin'
> I got to keep movin'
> blues falling down like hail
> blues falling down like hail
> Ummmmmmmmmmmmmmmmmm
> blues falling down like hail
> blues falling down like hail
> And the days keeps on worrying me
> there's a hell hound on my trail
> hell hound on my trail
> hell hound on my trail

When the song was concluded, one might have expected the singer to be enveloped in a swirling mist, but instead Robert Johnson, a modern-day Orpheus perhaps who struggled against the urge to look back, went on to perform two takes of "Little Queen of Spades" and his two additional reworkings of Lonnie Johnson material before taking up a more original theme once again with "Me and the Devil Blues."

Robert Johnson left the recording studio on Sunday, June

20, 1937. By Johnny Shines's recollections he hooked up with Shines just afterward in Red Water, Texas. "We worked Texas until the cold weather began to set in, then we headed for the southern part of Texas. That's when I found out that Texas was a cotton country; I had thought Texas was only a cow country. Robert and I came back into Arkansas as far as Little Rock. I can't recall just what happened, but my mother was in Arkansas not too far from Hughes, and I ended up there. Robert went on, but I stayed on in Hughes. One night I came in and was putting my

*Juke joint outside Clarksdale on a Saturday night,*
*November 1939.*

MARION POST WOLCOTT. LIBRARY OF CONGRESS, FSA.

⟦ 46 ⟧

guitar away when a girl came up to me and told me that a fellow was in my bed who said he knew me real well and could play like she had never heard before. When she said guitar, that did it! I knew it was Robert."

The last year of his life is speculation, probably not much different than the years that preceded it. He and Johnny Shines traveled to St. Louis perhaps and to Illinois, where, stranded in a little town which had never seen blacks before, they were asked to play a number. "So Robert starts out playing and me right with him, and they tried to get us to stay there, so we stayed a couple of nights, and the people at that time paid twenty-five cents a head, but we found out that the admission was not for music but to see our skin. You see, they had never seen a colored man before. We didn't want to be part of a freak sideshow. The guy thought we wanted more money, but we just wanted to get the hell out of there. After all, a man have pride. What is it to sell his pride for a few pennies?"

Robert spent time in Memphis. He returned to Helena and Robert Lockwood's mother. He traveled all through the Delta in Mississippi and Arkansas. He didn't hear from Ernie Oertle again, but that was not surprising. His records continued to be released, and at the time of his death at least six were in print. There is an unsubstantiated rumor that in the months before he died, he was playing with a band—including a pianist, a drummer, maybe even a horn player—which might not be all that unlikely since Muddy Waters was playing regularly with a string band at the time and Son House occasionally employed a friend named Little Buddy Sankfield on trombone, but which would alter our perception of Robert Johnson's music nonetheless. He was playing for get-backs and juke joints, house rent parties and country frolics, out in the streets and in wide-open riverfront saloons. Robert Johnson was an accomplished professional musician.

Then suddenly Robert left again. When I caught up with him, it was in St. Louis. He left me again in St. Louis, and I caught up with him again in Helena. If you want to guess, you can score yourself a hundred: yes, he was back with Robert Lockwood's mother again. Then Robert went over into Mississippi; I didn't like the thought of Mississippi, so I didn't go with him, and I never saw Robert again.

—JOHNNY SHINES

I went to Mississippi with Robert that time he got hurt by a truck, and we stayed in Tutwiler. I was part of the cause of Robert getting hit, because I was not going to go in that direction. I was fixing to go back home. And he turned around, and backing up, turning around, he slipped off the fender of the truck and fell under it. I stayed around for three or four days until he got well, but I just decided I wouldn't be with him no more.

—ROBERT JR. LOCKWOOD

I hung around with Robert about two years, off and on. Last time me and him was together we was coming out of Memphis. I was going my way to Robinsonville, and he was on his way to Greenwood. . . .

—HOWLIN' WOLF

So he left and went out there from Greenwood, Mississippi. The next word we heard was from his mother, who told us he was dead.

—SON HOUSE

He was poisoned three miles from Greenwood, Mississippi. He was playing for a country dance, but he was living in Greenwood at the time. About 2:00 he got so sick they had to bring him back to town . . . and he died in Greenwood [and] was buried out from Greenwood out at a place called Three Forks, not far from where he was playing

—DAVID "HONEYBOY" EDWARDS
in an interview with Pete Welding,
published in 1968

There were many stories about Johnson's death over the years, many linking it with his presumed pact with the devil. Son House said in 1965: "We never did get the straight of it. We first heard that he got stabbed to death. Next, a woman poisoned him, and then we heard something else. We never did get the straight of it." Johnny Shines heard that Robert had been poisoned and "crawled on his hands and knees and barked like a dog before he died." Others heard that he lingered for days and suggested that he had been struck down by the black arts, his note finally come due. Nothing was known for certain, however, aside from the fact of his death in 1938, when Ernie Oertle went looking for him, until in 1968 Gayle Dean Wardlow discovered a death certificate that proved he had indeed died in Greenwood and actually provided an estimated age at death. At the same time Mack McCormick pursued the lead furnished in Honeyboy Edwards's interview (Edwards, a protégé of Robert Johnson and Big Joe Williams, moved to Chicago in 1939 and recorded there in the early fifties but was, ironically, discovered back in Mississippi by Library of Congress researcher Alan Lomax while he was tracing the roots of Robert Johnson's music in 1941) and independently uncovered both the death certificate and the first solid leads on the mysterious death of Robert Johnson.

At a lonely country crossroads, McCormick says, he came across a man who, while himself refusing to speak of it, gave the names of two eyewitnesses to Johnson's murder. These witnesses lived in Indianapolis and Flint, Michigan, and in early 1970 McCormick followed up by locating and interviewing them. "The accounts agreed substantially as to the motive, the circumstances, and in naming the person responsible for the murder. It had been a casual killing that no one took very seriously. In their eyes Robert Johnson was a visiting guitar player who got murdered."

McCormick duly reported his findings to the LeFlore County sheriff who was "astonished at being handed a thirty-one-year-old murder" but, not surprisingly, was not much interested in pursuing "the circumstances of the crime." It was this discovery, however, that set McCormick off in earnest in pursuit of the other details of Robert Johnson's life. "The account of the murder seemed as though it should be the last chapter in a biography. What remained was to find the people and information that would become the other chapters, those that would give us some understanding of his life and circumstances. Somehow learning about his death obligated me to go the rest of the distance."

*Dirt road, March 1939.*
MARION POST WOLCOTT. LIBRARY OF CONGRESS, FSA.

Evidently, in August 1938, Johnson was playing at a dance in Three Forks, some fifteen miles out of Greenwood, as Honeyboy Edwards suggested. He and Honeyboy had been playing out there for several weeks running, by Honeyboy's account.

> A fellow give a dance, he lived in the country, but he come to the little city and picked the boys up out of the little city and carry them back in the country and play on a Saturday and Friday night. And when we get through, they'd bring us back in our old cars, back to town where we lived at.

How I got it, this fellow said Robert was messing around with his wife or something like that. So Robert came back to Greenwood and went back the next Saturday night out there. So he gave some of his friends some whiskey to give Robert to drink—I was lucky I didn't drink none of the whiskey, but I don't guess they was trying to give it to me. His friend give it to Robert—you see, he give it to him to drink because he had it in for Robert and his wife. But he still kept him to play for him! I think this fellow was named Ralph.

. . . About 1:00 Robert taken sick when he was playing. All the people just came out the city said they wanted him to play, 'cause they was drinking and all them having a good time, and they was begging him to play, and he played sick. And they said he told the public, he said, "Well, I'm sick, y'all see, but I'm playing, but I'm still sick. I'm not able to play." About 2:00 he got so sick they had to bring him back to town. . . .

This pretty much corresponds with the bare bones of the story McCormick has given out to date. By both accounts Robert Johnson lay dying for several days, and toward the end he wrote something on a piece of paper. He was buried in the graveyard of a small church near Morgan City, outside of Greenwood, in an unmarked grave. "You may bury my body," he had sung, "down by the highway side / So my old evil spirit can catch a Greyhound bus and ride."

The news traveled throughout the Delta and up to Memphis all through the next few weeks. One day Robert's sister,

Carrie, opened the door of her Georgia Street home and saw her son Louis standing there with Robert's guitar. "Son, where's Uncle Robert?" McCormick reports she said. "And he said, 'He's dead, Mama.'" Louis had been down in Mississippi, where Julia had told him the news and handed him the guitar to bring back to Memphis and give to Robert's brother, Charles Leroy. Julia had learned by phone, Carrie said, in the Delta, where she was living separated from her new husband, a preacher. Word then spread all through the family clusters, with a time lag of perhaps six months to a year before everyone had learned the fact of Robert Leroy Johnson's death, and with the story undoubtedly undergoing many transformations in the process. Ernie Oertle, who himself died the following year (thus cutting off the one direct line the outside world had to the lineage of Robert Johnson), started looking for Johnson in the late fall of 1938 at Don Law's direction. John Hammond wanted to present Johnson at his historic "From Spirituals to Swing" concert at Carnegie Hall in December. Law protested that this was a grave mistake, that Johnson would probably be scared to death—by all accounts, not a very accurate reading of Johnson's character but one which probably tells a lot about his demeanor around whites. In any case, Oertle quickly found out that Johnson was dead, and his replacement on the Carnegie Hall stage was Big Bill Broonzy. Hammond announced the death just prior to the concert in an enthusiastic, if somewhat impressionistic, elegy (which appeared in the December 13 issue of *New Masses*, the sponsor of the event) and he played recordings of "Walkin' Blues" and "Preachin' Blues" from the stage in tribute. Sporadic interest was expressed in Johnson over the years, primarily by blues and jazz collectors, and his

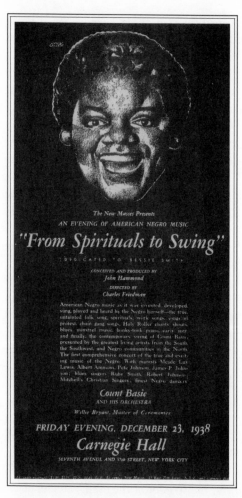

*From the* New Masses, *December 13, 1938.*
*( Robert Johnson's name is at far right, next-to-last line. )*

COURTESY OF PAUL GARON.

music never really disappeared from sight, unlike, say, the very rare recordings of Charley Patton or Son House, which became accessible on a mass level only in the sixties. It was not until the death certificate was discovered—and then in March of 1972 Mack McCormick reached Robert's half-sister Bessie on the telephone, after diligently combing telephone books and city directories from the Second World War on in Baltimore, Virginia, Maryland, and Memphis—that any part of the myth was actually substantiated. Almost numbed by the sheer drudgery of his search, McCormick put the familiar question to her and, only half-listening for a response, heard her say, "Oh, you mean my baby brother, Robert?"

WHAT HAVE WE GOT, then, when all is said and done? A few "facts," indistinguishable, really, from the "facts" of many bluesmen's lives. Some anecdotes, embellished perhaps over the years. A portrait of a young man who "didn't talk too much," was "moody," was perceived by whites as unsure of himself and by his peers as a rambler, a showman, but a "lone wolf" who, in Johnny Shines's words, was "close only to his own guitar." He was "friendly," he was "neat," he spoke little about his family or his past (but then, one wonders, who did?), he was well-liked but little-known. Perhaps the best summation comes in Johnny Shines's description of his friend as "very bashful but very imposing." Polite, self-effacing unreadable—destined to remain as much of a mystery, as much of a phantom, in Mack McCormick's conceit, as he was before a single fact was known or a single document unearthed.

The sources of his art will likewise remain a mystery.

The parallels to Shakespeare are in many ways striking. The towering achievement. The shadowy presence. The critical dissent that great art cannot come from a person so uneducated. The way in which each could cannibalize tradition and create a synthesis that is certainly recognizable in its sources and yet somehow altogether and wholly original. I am not arguing that Robert Johnson's art has a Shakespearean scope; nor is he a lost figure in an epic tradition, as some romanticists would suggest. As a lyric poet, though, he occupies a unique position where he can very much stand on his own.

His music remains equally unique. Not that it cannot be placed within a definable tradition, vigorously carried on by Muddy Waters and Johnny Shines, among others. But there was something about his music that seemed to strike all who listened, so that even a professional musician like Henry Townsend—on friendly terms with recording stars like Roosevelt Sykes and Lonnie Johnson—would express his awe at Robert's technique and execution. Most accounts agree he rarely practiced. "When he picked up his guitar, he picked it up for business," says Johnny Shines. According to both Shines and Robert Lockwood he was extremely reluctant to expose new material in public. Women with whom he stayed described to Mack McCormick how they would wake up in the middle of the night to discover him fingering the guitar strings almost soundlessly at the window by the light of the moon. If he realized that they were awake, he would stop almost immediately, a detail which corresponds with the many accounts of how he would shield his hands or turn away if he felt that another musician's eyes were on him while he was playing. He liked to play solo for the most part,

*A young Muddy Waters. Chess publicity shot, late 1940s.*

though Townsend describes working out parts with him and Johnny Shines says that on certain songs he welcomed a complement and had decided ideas of what part he wanted the second guitar to play. Most observers agree that he generally played his songs the same way each time; it might be that before he had a song worked out he would experiment with different voicings, but for the most part, once the song was set, neither accompaniment nor vocal effects varied a great deal. His was a very clearly thought-out approach, then, but where he got his initial conception from no one seems to know. "He was a great guy for plain inspiration," Henry Townsend told Pete Welding. "He'd get a feeling, and out of nowhere he could put a song together. . . . I remember asking him about songs he had sung two or three nights before, and he'd tell me, well, he wouldn't, he couldn't do that one again. And I'd ask him why. He'd say, 'Well, that was just a feeling. I was just, just . . . reciting from a feeling.'"

What made his music so different from that of his contemporaries is equally a mystery. You can point to Hambone Willie Newbern, whose "Rollin' and Tumblin'" melody (actually a traditional piece, which was first recorded by Newbern) was the inspiration for many of Johnson's songs; you can point to Son House, Johnson's closest influence, or Charley Patton, an equally emotive performer. The music of more apparently sophisticated guitarists like Scrapper Blackwell and, of course, Lonnie Johnson, shows up again and again in his work, and his style of slide guitar playing was a commonplace in the Delta. And yet there was something altogether unique and immediately recognizable about the way in which Robert Johnson transmuted all these familiar elements, adapted them to the nervous, edgy style that critic Whitney Balliett once called "rough" and "wild-animal"-like. Perhaps this was the very source of his attraction: the seeming tension between a fiery emotionalism barely on the edge of control and a masterful sense of technique. Johnny Shines has been most eloquent in describing the effect of his music as well as its accomplishments. According to Shines: "Robert came along with the walking bass, the boogie bass, and using diminished chords that were not built in one form. He'd do rundowns and turnbacks, going down to the sixth and seventh. He'd do repeats. None of this was being done. . . . I guess the guitar players before Robert come along just picked up what their daddies had done. It was like father, like son. Robert said, to heck with father, he'd do it the way he wanted to." And yet for all of his regard for Robert's technical accomplishments, which, while undoubtedly real, could very likely have been duplicated by any number of guitar adepts, even Johnny Shines recognizes that the real uniqueness of his music lay in its emotional appeal.

"He was a guy," Johnny wrote in his own reminiscence of Robert, "that could find a way to make a song sound good with a slide regardless of its contents or nature. His guitar seemed to talk—repeat and say words with him like no one else in the world could. . . . This sound affected most women in a way that I could never understand. One time in St. Louis we were playing one of the songs that Robert would like to play with someone once in a great while, 'Come On In My Kitchen.' He was playing very slow and passionately, and when we had quit, I noticed no one was saying anything. Then I realized they were crying—both women and men."

His voice, too, served as the ideal emotional conveyance. Not as heavy as House's or Muddy Waters's, for example, nor as forceful as Johnny Shines's, Robert Johnson's voice possessed a plasticity and an adaptability that lent itself to every variety of emotional effect. "It was not particularly strong," Johnny Shines says, "but it carried very well, he would sing loud and soft just for the effect of the song." You can hear this over and over in the recordings, which demonstrate a grasp of dynamics, a range of vocal effects that eludes attempts at electronic duplication. At times he seems virtually to be impersonating another, rougher singer, as he interjects a rough growl or aside; at other times he croons like the Bing Crosby records that he evidently admired, but with a sexual intensity that makes it seem as if he is crooning obscenities. What makes his work so unrepeatable is the way in which he intermixes all his approaches. At times his voice cracks, as if it really were slipping out of control; often he employs a tight, constricted vocal tone that effectively conveys this same tension. In one song he sings, "I been stuttering, oh-oh d-drive, oh oh d-drive my blues away." Occasionally you will hear a more full-throated vocal. At times he seems as free as Aretha Franklin or James Brown at their best, at other times as controlled as the most metronomic blues singer. Always, it seems, he is searching for a conscious effect.

Perhaps this very facility, this openness to new sounds and experimentation, would have led to a new kind of fusion music in the forties and fifties. Johnny Shines is convinced of it. "Robert's material was way ahead of his time," says Shines. "He was already trying to play jazz, you see, diminished sixths, diminished sevenths, all that kind of stuff that you *still* won't hear today. A lot of people think that if Robert was around today he'd still be playing the same thing, but he was playing stuff then that they're only catching up to now. If he was around today, you can't *imagine* what he'd be doing." Shines envisions a kind of Wes Montgomery progression, or perhaps something close to what Robert Jr. Lockwood plays today—a mix of swing, bebop and traditional blues—and perhaps this would have been the case. Or perhaps, like some of the less fortunate blues singers rediscovered in the sixties, in middle age he would have lost the edge off his singing voice, his playing would have become clumsy

and conventional, and he would have appeared a sad reminder, a near-parody of the great artist he once had been.
Unlike Shines and Lockwood he may not have been stable
enough to have survived the rigors and dislocations of meeting
a whole new audience which knew nothing, save what it had
read, of the background of his music. And yet in the end
none of this speculation really matters, for Robert Johnson,
like Housman's athlete, like Orpheus, Keats, and James
Dean, was kissed by the flame of youth and never lived to
see the effects of the infatuation wear off.

The news of his death hit the blues community hard.
Shines heard of it from Sonny Boy Williamson (Rice Miller),
who claimed that Johnson had died in his arms. Son House
obviously saw it as an inevitable denouement for a protégé
who simply would not take good advice. Robert Jr. Lockwood
gave up playing the guitar for a long time because he was so
affected and "because I didn't know nothing else but his
songs to play." And yet the songs were kept alive, in many
cases by musicians who had only casually known Robert
Johnson or—in the case of Muddy Waters—known *of* Johnson. Did they speak of him? I ask Robert Jr. and Johnny
Shines. When they sang his songs, did they unconsciously
nod toward his memory? Did friends ever get together in the
course of an evening and exchange reminiscences? "Some
did, some didn't," Shines says, but, from what he and Robert
say, for the most part they didn't. Robert Johnson's music
was an unacknowledged presence in the lives of a whole
generation of Mississippi-born musicians. They in turn
passed it on to the world. Robert Jr. Lockwood recorded
"Dust My Broom" for Mercury in November 1951, several
months before Elmore James, another of Johnson's disciples,

*The King Biscuit Boy: Robert Jr. Lockwood singing for King Biscuit Flour, early 1940s.*

MAX MOORE. COURTESY OF MIKE ROWE / BLUES UNLIMITED.

had a national hit with the same song (with Sonny Boy Williamson accompanying him on harmonica) on the Trumpet label. Johnny Shines did an unreleased session for Columbia in 1946 which featured several songs very much in the Robert Johnson tradition. Baby Boy Warren, who knew Johnson in Memphis, recorded "Stop Breakin' Down" around 1954, though a good part of the inspiration may have come from the first Sonny Boy Williamson's well-known adaptation. Honeyboy Edwards, along with a whole raft of others, recorded "Sweet Home Chicago" in 1952 or 1953 and continued to mine the vein of Robert Johnson material available to him. And, of course, Muddy Waters, through his popular Chess recordings, constantly drew upon the inspiration ("Mean Red Spider," "Streamline Woman") and repertoire ("Walkin' Blues," "Kind Hearted Woman") of Robert Johnson.

Just how unaware this school of blues singers, in touch with each other yet only tangentially, was of the massive interest building in the outside world is indicated by the response of Calvin Frazier, Johnny Shines's cousin (with whom Shines and Johnson traveled to Detroit and broadcast on the Elder Moten Hour in 1937–38), when collector George Paulus found him still living in Detroit in the late sixties. "Did you ever hear of Robert Johnson?" Frazier asked Paulus then. "Calvin's description of Robert," Paulus wrote, "was of a man who was moody and quickly changing emotions. Robert, he said, was crazy, because he was so involved with music. . . . Calvin said he never heard any of Robert's records, so on a following visit I brought along an LP. 'Mother-fucker . . . that Robert!' Calvin explained, as the disc played on, he did not even know there was an LP of a little-known figure like Johnson. He said he did not imagine I had ever known about Johnson; so he thought he would tell me about his favorite musician."

Like Joe Hill, in a sense, Robert Johnson never died; he simply became an idea. Robert Jr. Lockwood had one last flash of Johnson after his death. He was playing in Handy Park in Memphis one day probably a couple of years after Johnson had died, and a man walked up to him "and stood and just looked at me play and just stood there, and I knew he must have been doing that, you know, from some sort of concern. So finally I stopped playing, and he said, 'You're Robert Jr., aren't you?' I said, 'Yes.' He said, 'I live right around the corner. Would you go home with me? I got something I want to show you.' Well, I told him, 'Yeah,' and I walked around there, and he reached in the closet and got out a guitar. It was a Kalamazoo, big round-hole, made by Gibson. He said, 'You know this guitar?' I said, 'Yeah. It look like Robert's.' He said, 'It is.' And he told me he was one of Robert's brothers. I took the guitar and set down and played it and handed it back to him. I ain't seen him since."

PIECES OF A PUZZLE, tantalizing clues—perhaps Mack McCormick's *Biography of a Phantom* will elucidate the mystery, but the title alone seems to belie this intent. It will undoubtedly provide more facts, supply more anecdotes, and fill out our picture of the times, but the central mystery of Robert Johnson will remain. For McCormick sees, too, a figure of intriguing illusion and common clay, the most prosaic fact and symbolic fiction, a man who, as Calvin Frazier and others have suggested, was consumed by his art but no more or less consumed than the middle-class poets, painters, filmmakers who seem so much more familiar to us today.

Not even the pictures, which McCormick first uncovered in 1972 and which are just now, more than fifteen years later, beginning to see the light of day, speak in an undiluted voice. These in a sense were the grail; for so long they seemed as if they must be some sort of Rosetta stone, the final verification that there was indeed a Robert Johnson who existed in the flesh and was not a construct of some collector-fantasist's imagination. At the time of our original meeting, in 1976, McCormick shows me four pictures (there is a fifth, the formal portrait of Robert Johnson with guitar at the front of this book, which I will not see until a couple of years later). Before he will explain the pictures to me, McCormick puts me through a kind of catechism, asking me to elucidate on my perceptions of each unidentified photograph that I study searching for clues. I survey the faces, trying to read into them aspects of the story that I already know or that McCormick has just told me. Yes, McCormick confirms, that is Julia, Robert's mother, eyes half-closed, Sunday-go-to-meeting hat perched firmly atop her head, feet planted solidly on the ground, looking every inch the iron-willed matriarch. Yes, it's possible to imagine her answering the telephone in some hot little Delta town only to hear that her youngest son is dead. It's more difficult to imagine her moving from labor camp to labor camp or to get a sense of her fall, from the property-owning wife of Charles Dodds to the disgraced mistress of Noah Johnson, who may have been the most enterprising of men but who is always described somewhat dismissively, like Robert Johnson's stepfather, Dusty Willis, as a "fieldhand."

The next picture is of Robert's brother, Charles Leroy, looking sharp and dapper in a creased hat, jacket, and tie, legs crossed languidly, much like the studio shot of Robert, cradling a guitar that his brother might have played. There is a woman beside him in the picture, evidently his wife, wearing a coat and hat herself, looking pretty and expectant.

The next photograph shows a young man in a sailor's uniform, obviously pleased, obviously proud, with another

*Julia Major(s) Dodds, ca. 1912.*
COURTESY OF STEVE LAVERE, © 1989.

man, very slightly older, standing beside him, his arm draped affectionately around the sailor's shoulder. The sailor, Mack McCormick tells me, is Robert's nephew, Louis, at home in Memphis, on his first leave from the Navy base in Norfolk, where he was stationed in 1936–37. Later he would be transferred up to Annapolis, and that was how his mother Carrie and his aunt Bessie would eventually move up to the Maryland area, where McCormick found them. Louis was very close to his uncle, and in fact, when McCormick visited Carrie in 1972, was so disturbed by the conversation that he retreated into his room and refused to come out.

And the other man in the picture? The man in the sharp pin-striped suit? That, of course, is Robert Johnson. I stare and stare at the picture, study it, scrutinize it, seek to memorize it, and for my very efforts am defeated. What is there in this face, this expression; what can you read into a photograph? The man has short nappy hair; he is slight, one foot is raised, and he is up on his toes as though stretching for height. There is a sharp crease in his pants, and a handkerchief protrudes from his breast pocket—real or imaginary, I'm no longer sure; perhaps it would be more accurate to say that the *image* of a handkerchief protrudes. His eyes are deep-set, reserved, his expression forms a half-smile, there seems to be a gentleness about him, his fingers are extraordinarily long and delicate, his head is tilted to one side. That is all. There may well be more, but that is all I can remember. I try to combine this with what I know of Johnson, what McCormick has told me. I read volumes into his relationship with Louis and imagine Louis coming home from Mississippi with his uncle's guitar. Johnny Shines's description to John Earl of Johnson himself comes to mind.

"His shoulders were carried high with a little pitch forward. His sharp, slender fingers fluttered like a trapped bird. . . . The cataract in his left eye was immediately noticeable to anyone. . . ." I look at the photo again and try to imagine the warmth and magnetism of the man, but in the end I am not really sure if anything is revealed.

There is a final picture, of a man dressed in khakis, looking very much like Robert Johnson, but too old, too contemporary. I ask McCormick about this picture. This, he explains, is Robert Johnson's son, one of a number of children whom McCormick found and interviewed. He was thirty-nine when the picture was taken in 1970, a businessman in a rural community, whose mother—sixteen at the time of his birth—moved in with an aunt after Robert moved on. The expression on his face is identical to that of his father, except that there does not seem to be that hint of disturbance about the eyes. Gentleness, reserve, hurt perhaps—but not the glint of pain. For him and for all of Robert Johnson's heirs—legal, not musical or spiritual—the question of Johnson's rediscovery seems not so much an artistic as a practical matter, perhaps a proud, perhaps a painful reminder of another time, another age, raising only the question that was voiced to McCormick: "Is there anything coming from my daddy's records?" For them the real Robert Johnson exists lodged firmly in memory. For the rest of us he remains to be invented.

ACKNOWLEDGMENTS AND
BIBLIOGRAPHY

First I'd like to acknowledge the trailblazing work of Mack McCormick, whose research is obviously the basis for much of this essay. A great deal of the information included here is based on my interview with him in 1976, when publication of his book, *Biography of a Phantom*, seemed imminent. The book, when it appears, will, I am sure, fill in many of the gaps and should prove an enduring classic.

In addition, the work of David Evans and Pete Welding in particular has been an invaluable aid in offering both historical insights and cultural perspective and providing—in Welding's interview with Honeyboy Edwards—the basis for my account of Robert Johnson's death. I'd like to thank Robert Lockwood and Johnny Shines as well for all their help, even *after* all the other interviews they had done. Johnny Shines's words have proved an especially eloquent guide to the world of Robert Johnson, and while I have interviewed Johnny a good number of times myself over the years, I think the perceptive reader will note that I have in some cases combined quotes from different interviews—by myself, Jack Viertel, Pete Welding, Mark Humphrey, Bob Rusch, and John Earl—in order to provide a fuller account of a particular moment or expand on a particular thought. I have done my best in these instances to maintain a consistent account and a steady tone, but if there is any lapse in accuracy due to this method, it should be charged to me, not to Johnny Shines. One other note that seems worth mentioning: dates are often impressionistic in stories that are themselves unassailable, so here, too, I have done my best to apply common sense and logic to create a chronology that squares with the various accounts.

The following is a selected bibliography of some of the written work which has been helpful in preparing this essay. In addition, I have included a small number of significant books and articles that have been published since this piece was written. I've tried to list everything that was of substantive aid, but if I have left out an obvious source, it is due not to intention but to the inherent difficulties of attempting to retrace one's steps some time after the work is finished.

### BOOKS

Samuel Charters. *The Bluesmen*. New York: Oak Publications, 1967.

———. *The Country Blues*. New York: Rinehart, 1959.

———. *Robert Johnson*. New York: Oak Publications, 1972.

David Evans. *Tommy Johnson*. London: Studio Vista, 1971.

David Evans. *Big Road Blues*. Berkeley: University of California Press, 1982

John Fahey. *Charley Patton*. London: Studio Vista, 1970.

Alan Greenberg. *Love In Vain*. New York: Doubleday/Dolphin, 1983.

Bob Groom. *Robert Johnson*. Knutsford, U.K., *Blue World*, 1967 (revised edition 1969).

———. *Charlie Patton*. Knutsford, U.K., *Blues World*, 1969.

Peter Guralnick. *Feel Like Going Home* (revised edition). New York: Harper & Row, 1989.

John Hammond, *On Record*. New York: Summit Boooks, 1977.

Greil Marcus. *Mystery Train*. New York: Dutton, 1975.

Paul Oliver. *Conversation With the Blues*. London: Cassell, 1965.

Robert Palmer. *Deep Blues*. New York: Viking, 1981.

Jeff Todd Titon. *Early Downhome Blues*. Urbana: University of Illinois Press, 1977.

Al Wilson. *Son House: An Analysis of His Music and a Biography*. Bexhill-on-Sea, U.K., *Blues Unlimited* Collectors Classics 14, 1966.


ARTICLES, INTERVIEWS AND LINER NOTES

Whitney Balliett. Review of Robert Johnson album. *New Yorker*, Nov. 3, 1962.

Stephen Calt. "Robert Johnson Recapitulated." *Blues Unlimited* 86, Nov. 1971.

Stephen Cicchetti. "Blues Wizard's San Antonio Legacy." San Antonio *Express-News*, Nov. 30, 1986.

John Cowley. "Walking Blues." *Blues Unlimited* 106, Feb./ Mar. 1974.

————. Liner notes to *Walking Blues*. Flyright LP 541.

————. "Really The 'Walking Blues.'" *Juke Blues* 1, July 1985.

William Cummerow. "Living Blues Interview: Robert Jr. Lockwood." *Living Blues* 12, Spring 1973.

Frank Driggs. Liner notes to *Robert Johnson: King of the Delta Blues Singers*. Columbia LP 1654.

John Earl. "A Lifetime in the Blues: Johnny Shines." *Blues World* 46/49, 1973.

David Evans. "Blues on Dockery's Plantation: 1895 to 1967."
　　*Blues Unlimited* 49–50, Jan. and Feb. 1968.

———. "The Fiddling Joe Martin Story." *Blues World* 20,
　　July 1968.

———. "Son House: Some Further Comments." *Blues Un-
　　limited* 43, May 1967.

———. "Interview with Henry Speir." *JEMF Quarterly* 8,
　　1972.

Tim Ferris. "Robert Johnson." *Rolling Stone*, Feb. 4, 1971.

Bob Groom. "Robert Johnson: The Man Behind the Music."
　　*Blues World* 5, Nov. 1965.

———. "Robert Johnson Revisited." *Blues World* 2, May
　　1965.

———. "Son House at Lancaster University." *Blues World*
　　33, Aug. 1970.

———. "Standing at the Crossroads: Robert Johnson's Re-
　　cordings." *Blues Unlimited* 118–121, Mar.–Oct. 1976.

Peter Guralnick. "In Search of Robert Johnson." *Rolling
　　Stone*, Mar. 26, 1976.

John Hammond. "Jim Crow Blues." *New Masses*, Dec. 13,
　　1938 (Courtesy of Paul Garon).

Mark Humphrey. "Johnny Shines: A Living Legacy of Delta
　　Blues." *Frets Magazine*, Nov. 1979.

Bruce Iglauer. "Reconstructing Robert Johnson." *Living
　　Blues* 5, Summer 1971.

Julius Lester. "I Can Make My Own Songs: An Interview
　　with Son House." *Sing Out!*, Vol. XV, No. 3, 1965.

———. "'Mister White, Take a Break': An Interview with
　　Bukka White." *Sing Out!*, Vol. XVIII, No. 4, 1968.

Chris Lornell. Liner notes to *Sittin' on Top of the World*.
　　Biograph LP 12044.

Greil Marcus. "When You Walk in the Room." *The Village Voice*, Dec. 9, 1986.

Robert Palmer. "Robert Jr. Lockwood: Outlaw Blues," *Rolling Stone*, Mar. 22, 1979.

George Paulus. "Motor City Blues and Boogie" (including an interview with Calvin Frazier). *Blues Unlimited* 85, Oct. 1971.

"The Rock and Roll Hall of Fame: Forefathers." First known publication of any photograph of Robert Johnson. *Rolling Stone*, Feb. 13, 1986.

Bob Rusch and Mike Joyce. "Johnny Shines: Interview." *Cadence*, Feb. 1978.

Johnny Shines. "Remembering Robert Johnson." *American Folk Music Occasional* 2, Oak Publications, 1970.

Mit Schuller. "Robert Jr. Lockwood: Master of the Blues." *Guitar Player*, Nov. 1975.

Gayle Dean Wardlow. "Legends of the Lost: The Story of Henry Speir." *Blues Unlimited* 31, 34–36, 1966.

———. "Son House: Comments and Additions." *Blues Unlimited* 42, Mar./Apr. 1967.

Dick Waterman. "Obituary for Son House." *Living Blues* 84, Jan./Feb. 1989.

Pete Welding. "Hellhound on his Trail: Robert Johnson." *down beat*, Music '66.

———. "'I Sing for the People': An Interview with Howlin' Wolf." *down beat*, Dec. 14, 1967.

———. "Interview with David 'Honeyboy' Edwards." *Blues Unlimited* 54, June 1968.

———. "Interview with Muddy Waters." *American Folk Music Occasional* 2, Oak Publications, 1970.

————. Liner notes to *Down on Stovall's Plantation*. Testament LP 2210.

————. Liner notes to *Robert Johnson: King of the Delta Blues Singers Vol. 2*. Columbia LP C 30034.

————. "Ramblin': Johnny Shines." *Living Blues* 22, 23, Jul./Aug., Sept./Oct. 1975.

————. "'The Robert Johnson I Knew': An Interview with Henry Townsend." *down beat*. Oct. 31, 1968.

## ROBERT JOHNSON AND HIS MUSIC: A SELECTED DISCOGRAPHY

Probably the logical place to start is with Robert Johnson himself, though this is not the beginning, nor the end, certainly, of any appreciation of his music. There are, of course, two essential albums on Columbia that have been available for years: *King of the Delta Blues Singer* Vols. I and II (Columbia 1654 and 30034). These consist of all twenty-nine of his individual recorded titles, along with three alternate takes. Nine additional alternate takes exist, all of which have been issued in different combinations on various collector LPs over the years (eight of them are currently available on *Mississippi Country Blues* Vol. I on the Austrian Document label). All forty-one variants are to be brought together in a single multi-album set which Columbia has once again scheduled, after more than a dozen years of delays, for the winter of 1989–1990. In the absence of any new titles being discovered (and Mack McCormick has in fact stated that there is at least one unissued, and unheard, side extant, "an extremely bawdy song that [Robert] did just for the enjoyment of the engineers"), this should be the definitive document.

So far as other sources of recorded material go, the following should give a good idea both of the sources of Robert Johnson's art and of his legacy.

### INFLUENCES

*The Roots of Robert Johnson* (Yazoo 1073). This covers just about every major influence on Robert's music, from Lonnie Johnson's slick urban stylings to Kokomo Arnold's original "Milk Cow Blues" to Skip James's dark falsetto moans and the Mississippi Sheiks' bittersweet "Sitting On Top of the World." The extensive notes make a very convincing musicological case for the direct link in each case between the original inspiration and Johnson's own individuated blues.

*Charley Patton: Founder of the Delta Blues* (Yazoo 1020). The subtitle suggests the reason that this is essential. It is not so much that Patton's style was directly assimilated into Robert's music (it was by contrast the clear antecedent of Howlin Wolf's) as that it represents the principal recorded documentation of first-generation Delta blues. Patton was coarse where Robert was refined, ferocious where Robert was sly, and overwhelming in his overall effect. This twenty-eight cut double album, which includes church songs, snatches of popular hits of the day, and pre-blues ballads as well as blues is the definitive selection, with the best sound (which is not saying much unless you listen to some of the other attempts at remastering) that we are ever likely to get.

*Son House: The Legendary 1941–1942 Recordings* (Folk Lyric 9002) and *Walking Blues* (Flyright 541). These are the recordings House did for Alan Lomax and the Library of Congress when Lomax was researching the tradition of Robert Johnson. Son House was probably the most significant Delta influence on Robert Johnson (Johnson's "Walking Blues" was a direct adaptation of the House original), though his impact on the music of Muddy Waters, a more literal-minded stylistic disciple, was considerably more direct. House possessed a majestic voice and a searing, if limited, bottleneck technique. In Muddy Waters's words: "When I was a boy coming up, that man was king, *king*, you hear me? Folks came from miles around to hear that man play the blues." On the second album, on three selections, you will hear House backed by a driving little band that includes Leroy Williams on harmonica, Willie Brown on second guitar, and Fiddlin' Joe Martin on mandolin. There is the additional bonus of five unique and idiosyncratic numbers by David "Honeyboy" Edwards, a bluesman who recorded only sporadically over the next forty years but who comes across here as a spirited cross between Robert Johnson and Big Joe Williams, his two principal sources of inspiration.

*Really! The Country Blues* (Origin Jazz Library 1), *The Mississippi Blues* Vols. I and II (Origin Jazz Library 5 and 11). The seminal collections of Mississippi Delta blues, including Charley Patton, Tommy Johnson, Skip James, Bukka White, Willie Brown and one double-sided cut each of Son House's three glorious 1931 two-part commercial recordings. These six sides are available on a single album called *Giants of Country Blues* Vol. I on the Austrian Wolf label (Wolf 116), but the Origin compilations, which spearheaded the first country blues revival in 1961, are so strong, and so diverse, that you owe it to yourself to at least start with them. In addition, in 1988 an extraordinary cache of never-before-heard Paramount test pressings from 1929 and 1930 was released on the Wolf-subsidiary Document label (*Delta Blues* Vol. I, Document 532). It includes not only clean alternate takes of three Charley Patton songs but variants on a previously unknown title by Tommy Johnson and an extraordinary, long-rumored number by Son House, the original "Walkin' Blues." It would be hard to say that this, too, was not indispensable.

*Skip James: 1931* (Yazoo 1072). Like all the Yazoo albums, the best sound, the best packaging, the best-informed (if not always the best-expressed) liner notes. All eighteen of Skip James's 1931 sides that have been recovered to date. A few years ago, for all of my admiration for Skip James and my knowledge that Robert Johnson had adapted his "22-20 Blues," I would never have thought of connecting his eerie, wholly idiosyncratic style so directly, but Yazoo annotator Stephen Calt has convinced me. As much as we look to Robert Johnson for vivid, sometimes startling originality of expression, so Robert must have looked to the deep, almost unfathomable blues of Nehemiah "Skip" James.

*Tommy Johnson: 1928–30* (Wolf 104). Here the connection is not so direct, but the music is just as beautiful. Tommy Johnson, like his near-contemporary Charley Patton, was an extremely popular progenitor of the Delta blues style on which Robert Johnson grew up. This is music of almost incomparable lyric beauty.

*Blues Before Sunrise* (Portrait 44122, reissued from Columbia 1799), *Leroy Carr: 1930–1935* (Magpie 4407). Very similar compilation albums by Leroy Carr and Scrapper Blackwell with a certain amount of overlap. These are the only LPs by broadly popular blues singers of the day that I'm going to cite, though I could as easily list collections by Lonnie Johnson or Big Bill Broonzy. My reasoning is that while Lonnie Johnson provided very much of a technical blueprint for Robert's uptown side, it was a model that tended to overwhelm him: he didn't so much absorb Lonnie as copy him, and the results were probably Robert's weakest efforts ("Malted Milk," "Drunken Hearted Man"). Big Bill Broonzy was clearly listened to and more readily absorbed, but Broonzy himself was something of a stylistic disciple of the guitar-piano duets of Carr and Blackwell. With Carr and Blackwell you can hear the very direct sources of inspiration for some of Robert Johnson's greatest music. Songs like "Blues Before Sunrise," "Mean Mistreater Mama," "Hurry Down Sunshine (See What Tomorrow Bring)," and "How Long Blues" exercised an incalculable influence not just on Johnson but on an entire generation of musically adventurous rural blues players. Carr's mellifluous vocals and Blackwell's stinging single-string guitar work provided a model of down home urbanity that continues to attract in a manner that is lively, mournful, engaging, and poignant by turns, but never far removed from a sense of good fun.

CONTEMPORARIES

*I'm in the Highway, Man*: Calvin Frazier and Sampson Pittman (Flyright 542). Unmistakable overtones of Robert Johnson, with whom Frazier traveled (Calvin Frazier was Johnny Shines's cousin) in the year or two preceding these

1938 Library of Congress recordings. Here we catch a fascinating glimpse of yet another near-dustbin of history as we get variants on "Kind Hearted Woman" ("Double Crossing Woman"), "Terraplane" ("I'm in the Highway, Man"), and even a distant echo of "Honeymoon Blues" ("Lilly Mae") without any of the self-consciousness that historical retrospection would necessarily lend. Calvin Frazier wasn't anywhere near as talented as Robert Johnson, and these performances are relatively lifeless compared to Johnson's taut renditions, but this could as easily have *been* Robert Johnson, and the performances are beautiful nonetheless.

*Down On Stovall's Plantation*: Muddy Waters (Testament 2210). Another lesson in what might have been. These 1941–42 Library of Congress recordings, which stem from the same Alan Lomax field trip that unearthed Son House (in fact, Muddy pointed Lomax towards House) are so unmistakably in the Robert Johnson mold that one is almost stunned at the sheer fact of their existence. The album offers not only searing solo sides by the twenty-six-year-old fieldworker, who is listed by his real name of McKinley Morganfield in Library of Congress notes, but Muddy accompanied by a country string band that includes second guitar, mandolin, and Charley Patton's old partner, Henry "Son" Sims, on fiddle as well. Without any question great music in its own right, this is also history as it might have been written.

*Mississippi Blues* Vol. I (Document 519). In addition to the eight Robert Johnson alternate takes, this album showcases all four of Robert Jr. Lockwood's 1941 Robert Johnson-styled commercial recordings (including the classic "Little Boy Blue" and "Take a Little Walk With Me") as well as the first issued post-war version of "Dust My Broom."

[ 79 ]

## JOHNNY SHINES
## AND ROBERT JR. LOCKWOOD

*Johnny Shines and Robert Lockwood* (Flyright 563). The Shines is absolutely essential. This is music of astonishing power, intensity, and originality, consisting of Johnny's 1952–53 JOB sessions in their entirety. These are, to my mind, some of the greatest postwar sides in the Robert Johnson tradition, with inspired duets with harmonica virtuoso Walter Horton, brilliant slide playing, and consistently challenging, and surprising, lyrics. The Lockwood doesn't match the pre-war, or much of his later, work, but Shines's ten tracks are living testimony to the enduring tradition of the Delta blues.

*Chicago Blues/Today!* Vol. III (Vanguard 79218). Six tracks by Johnny, his first upon rediscovery by Mike Rowe and Sam Charters in 1965. Includes "Dynaflow Blues," his explosive recreation of Robert's "Terraplane" (which emerged as "Fish Tail" on the earlier JOB session), a moment of sheer exuberance that has seldom been matched on record. Johnny's later recordings for Testament (*Masters of Modern Blues* Vol. I, Testament 2212), Blue Horizon (*Last Night's Dream*, Blue Horizon 7-63212), Advent (*Johnny Shines*, Advent 2803), and Rounder (*Hey Ba-Ba-Re-Bop!*, Rounder 2020) are all eminently worthwhile and yield almost equal pleasures, but start with the Vanguard and the JOB sessions and allow them to inspire you.

*Contrasts* and *Does 12* (Trix 3307 and 3317): Robert Jr. Lockwood. Robert in his modern incarnation, with progressive, strongly jazz-tinged ideas that would be worthy of his stepfather. This, as Robert and Johnny see it, represents the logical extension of Robert Johnson's adventurous musical spirit. My friend Dick Shurman has also brought to my attention a 1982 tribute album called *Plays Robert and Robert* (Black & Blue 33.740), on which Lockwood plays some of his stepfather's and his own best-known songs in solo versions on amplified 12-string guitar.

### MUDDY WATERS

*More Real Folk Blues* (Chess 9278). A tribute, really, to the Son House/Robert Johnson Delta school. Recorded entirely in the late forties and early fifties and for the most part with only Little Walter's unamplified harmonica and Big Crawford's upright bass to accompany Muddy's elegiac slide guitar. Even on Muddy's hits you'll hear frequent, unmistakable echoes of the Delta, but here you get the music of Robert Johnson transported to Chicago with no diminution of majesty or power. This is music of the most direct emotional impact.

### ELMORE JAMES

*"Let's Cut It": The Very Best of Elmore James* (Ace 192). Elmore James was the man who made "Dust My Broom" into a national hit (in 1952), and then into a career. It's almost impossible to go wrong with Elmore, but check this one out first for the sound, the selection, and the overall ambience. Includes "Dust My Blues" (a variant on the original), "Blues Before Sunrise," "Standing at the Crossroads," and an amazing "Goodbye Baby," which brings to mind an improbable combination of Robert Johnson, Tampa Red, and Solomon Burke. As direct a link as you are going to find, without a

trace of self-consciousness about it—because, after all, this was Elmore James's music, too.

*Ridin' in the Moonlight* (Ace 52); *The Legendary Sun Performers: Howlin' Wolf* (Charly 30134) or *Cadillac Daddy: Memphis Recordings, 1952* (Rounder SS28) or *The Howlin' Wolf Masterworks* Vols. I and II (Japanese P-Vine PLP 6062, 6065). A little more out of the way perhaps, but how could one (or how could *I*) offer up a survey of Delta blues without including Wolf? I couldn't. All five of the albums listed above pre-date Wolf's Chicago hits and are as raw as anything that's ever come out of the recording studio. There is a great deal of duplication between the Rounder and Charly, and the Japanese albums include many of the same cuts as well as some additional ones—so keep a sharp consumer's eye on your purchases. There are, of course, any number of vocal references to Charley Patton, and Wolf's music is permeated with echoes of the Delta style that he and Robert Johnson learned in the juke joints and cotton fields, but mostly it is just inimitably, indivisibly The Original Howlin' Wolf And His Orchestra. Another must-buy—but then I don't know which of these albums that I've named from my point of view are not.

This is just a start. I hope it will lead you to any number of blues discoveries and experiences of your own. If your local record store doesn't stock this sort of music in any quantity or quality, try Down Home Music, 10341 San Pablo Avenue, El Cerrito, California 94530; Round Up Records, P.O. Box 154, Cambridge, Massachusetts 02140; or Red Lick

Records, P.O. Box 3, Porthmadog, Gwynedd, Wales, U.K. All three do extensive, world-wide mail-order business; all three put out regular catalogues which include listings and insightful reviews of all new releases and re-releases; and Down Home publishes a comprehensive blues catalogue, with pithy descriptions of every record listed, that is as useful a tool as any that I know for starting up a blues collection or keeping one going.